DECON STRUC TING DIGITAL

Rock - your Digital !

♥ Sh.

DECON STRUC TING

DIGITAL

SIMPLE WAYS

to *connect* with your *next-generation*
financial clients

SHERI FITTS

Advantage®

Published by Advantage, Charleston, South Carolina.
Member of Advantage Media Group.

ADVANTAGE is a registered trademark, and the Advantage colophon is a trademark of Advantage Media Group, Inc.

Printed in the United States of America.

ISBN: 978-1-59932-682-5
LCCN: 2016937080

Book design by Katie Biondo.

This publication is designed to provide accurate and authoritative information in regard to the subject matter covered. It is sold with the understanding that the publisher is not engaged in rendering legal, accounting, or other professional services. If legal advice or other expert assistance is required, the services of a competent professional person should be sought.

Advantage Media Group is proud to be a part of the Tree Neutral® program. Tree Neutral offsets the number of trees consumed in the production and printing of this book by taking proactive steps such as planting trees in direct proportion to the number of trees used to print books. To learn more about Tree Neutral, please visit **www.treeneutral.com**.

Advantage Media Group is a publisher of business, self-improvement, and professional development books and online learning. We help entrepreneurs, business leaders, and professionals share their Stories, Passion, and Knowledge to help others Learn & Grow. Do you have a manuscript or book idea that you would like us to consider for publishing? Please visit **advantagefamily.com** or call **1.866.775.1696**.

This book is dedicated to my dad, Lorne Anton Fitts.
He's the computer geek in my genes.

TABLE OF CONTENTS

INTRODUCTION

In the 1970s, my father was a computer programmer. Back then, computers took up a whole room, and anything being programmed in would be inserted into the machine on a punch card—piles of punch cards. Today we can hold more computing power in one hand than that roomful of hardware managed only a short lifetime ago.

Dad introduced me to technology when I was in middle school. I used to go to work with him on Saturdays. I'd sit and play around at the data-entry typewriters. The old keyboard sounds are still so distinctive. I honestly believe this exposure removed any fear of technology and all things computer. By the time I entered high school, I began to take technology for granted as an everyday part of life. As a summer job, I did data entry. In college, one of my work-study assignments was for the Environmental Protection Agency, using the first version of a Macintosh word processor. It just seemed that, in most every job, I naturally migrated to a position that had something to do with exploring new technology—hence, my early exploration of the social space.

Thanks to my dad, I'm a digital native who's found a home and a career in teaching financial advisors how to use social media. Today, as founder and CEO of ShoeFitts Marketing, I lead a team that uses our deep expertise in all things marketing and financial services to help organizations and advisors create unforgettable marketing programs. We push hard to think differently and step out of our jargon-filled language and build human-centered connections meant to drive sales and retain clients.

This book is for financial advisors and the financial community at large—investment consultants, insurance broker-dealers, mutual-fund companies, Certified Financial Planners™, and even bankers—who have yet to embrace the power of the digital arena. It's important for you to understand how the various tactics and platforms work together. You can make them work for you regardless of the size and scale of your organization or practice.

The information in this book will deconstruct the digital world for you. It is designed to help you establish a new approach for your marketing, one that will drive sales as the tsunami of baby-boomer money begins to shift to the new holders of wealth: women and millennials. You'll get an understanding of the simple steps to get started using social media and the digital realm in your sales and relationship-management efforts. You'll also be introduced to a variety of resources and ideas on how to use various platforms. And you'll find valuable insights into how everything works together.

It's entirely understandable if you feel overwhelmed by the thought of entering the world of social media and digital marketing. But once you understand how to use technology to your advantage, once you understand how the digital puzzle pieces fit together, I'm confident you'll begin to find intersections of marketing, social media, and sales beyond what you learn in this book.

In the digital world, there's an awesome opportunity to create value and to deepen relationships. This is even more imperative as regulatory changes will make the industry even more challenging and competitive. If you're going to carve your own space in the evolving landscape, you must understand the competitive advantage of brand and brand value. You can no longer scale your practice by doing one-on-one, grip-and-grin, old-school cold calling and networking.

Yes, it can be challenging to use social media tools and stay within the parameters set forth by regulators. While those constraints require a little creativity, they can also serve as gravity to ground your ideas. That's really what compliance is about; it's the gravity that levels the playing field as you expand and grow. And it is possible to remain conservative and compliant while using social media platforms effectively. Realistically, the two-way nature of the social sphere gives you opportunities to learn more about your clients and prospects. (Imagine what you could learn from their Facebook posts alone!)

My approach to digital marketing sweeps the path for sales by learning more about clients and prospects. And the social sphere greatly aids in this mission, if used correctly, by increasing *sales* and *retention*. Sales and retention will always be the drivers of a successful business.

There are many resources available in addition to this book. In fact, there's an overload of information about social media and the digital world—just not many in our world of financial services. This book's purpose is to help you begin to make sense of it all.

Nobody is born knowing this stuff. The way I have learned is by doing. If you just make a commitment to get started—with a few small steps—you too can be comfortable in no time. A favorite quote of mine? "A journey of a thousand miles begins with a single step."

CHAPTER ONE

Word of Mouse

Remember Martha? The Martha Stewart that originated today's hip and growing maker movement? She gave us the tools, advice, guidance, and inspiration to elevate every part of our home. When I bought my first home, I immediately ordered a subscription to her magazine, *Martha Stewart Living*. Martha (my subscription and love of all her works, of course, put me on a first-name basis with her) infused every bit of her marketing brilliance into her magazine. It was a slightly different size from that of any other magazine available, so it always stood out. The photographs were highly artistic, even when they focused on the most domestic elements. (Even cleaning materials looked stunning.)

Every month, I pored through the pages, dreaming about building my nest and enriching my life in the process. Should I paint my walls robin's egg blue or sage green? Even my cooking rose to a whole new level. Martha's attitude was always to imagine that with planning, industriousness, and some creative juices, anything was possible and would make life more beautiful. I made everything from homemade mustard to fennel-topped crackers. In fact, I still make her clove-and-cardamom-spiced apple butter each autumn and her cioppino every Christmas (minus the mussels).

After so many years of being inspired by Martha, the news in mid-2015 that Martha Stewart Living Omnimedia (MSLO) would be a thing of the past was a touch heartbreaking. And for the end to come with a degree of dishonor and personal humiliation for Martha made it even more disheartening. In June 2015, MSLO was sold to Sequential Brands for $353 million in cash—just 25 percent of what her brand was valued at in 1999 at her $1.8 billion initial public offering.[1] To make it worse, Sequential Brands is known for buying up once-bright brands and squeezing every last dollar out of them. I imagine the company will make short work of getting the most out of MSLO's existing distribution partners, which sell anything from high-end cooking gear to pet wear and American flags.

Clearly, there are more than a few factors contributing to the brand's decline: Stewart's jail time in 2005 and her five-year ban from the board of directors as required by the federal regulators are among the top contenders.

---

1 John Kell, "Martha Stewart just sold her media empire for a near-clearance price," Fortune, June 22, 2015, http://fortune.com/2015/06/22/martha--stewart-sold/.

However, one key theme arises as the various branding, marketing, and financial wizards who once thought Martha almost invincible try to make sense of her change in fortune: she never really embraced the digital space. As beautiful, innovative, and inspirational as her magazine was, she was not able to translate those qualities into an online presence.

Unfortunately, a large constituency of financial advisors are following Martha Stewart's missteps. They neglect their websites, their online presence, and their digital communications. They fail to see how social networking builds connections, increases credibility, develops thought leadership, and grows sales. They are ignoring the huge potential of Generation D (digital).

Generation D is an emerging and growing cross-generational cohort of seventy-five million investors, with more than $27 trillion in assets. Generation X makes up about 50 percent of the group, with boomers and millennials splitting the remainder.

Generation D is defined by its "deeply digital lifestyle." The people in this classification are well educated, socially savvy, active, and engaged investors with a healthy dose of skepticism for the financial services arena. This generation seeks to validate financial information with friends and social media connections *before* sitting down with a financial advisor.

If you've got no digital presence, you've got no slice of the $27 trillion pie.

No matter which demographic you serve, the fact remains: The Internet has disrupted the way we acquire information and interact with the world. It is shaping an entirely new idea of what's possible in financial services. Responding to the digital demand is no longer an option—it's a necessity. Martha learned that lesson just a touch too late.

A Different World

The web has forever shifted the way we communicate—there is no going back. Some folks have thrown in the towel, claiming they're too old or too late to the party. Granted, if you, as a novice, look at the digital ecosystem and how it all fits together, it looks horribly complicated. Thankfully, it's not as complicated as it seems, and there is still plenty of opportunity for you to differentiate yourself online, especially in our slow-to-adapt world of financial services. Think of it this way: you didn't know everything about financial services on day one; you grew your experience and expertise over time.

The digital space is no different, so you need to have the same mind-set. You're not going to be doing nothing one day and the next day have it all together and set the web on fire.

True, no one with a great amount of wealth heads to Google to find a financial advisor. While referrals are still the way many firms get business, the way referrals happen today is very, very different. With digital in the picture, most people aren't going to blindly go with a particular advisor solely on the advice of a friend. People will—and are—using online resources to research someone referred to them. They do their homework and show up to the conversation prepared. (Consider this statistic from CEB Global: buyers are already 57 percent through the purchase process before sales professionals even speak to them.[2]) Financial advisors who aren't online, who aren't embracing the digital realm, will miss out on these opportunities.

When I speak, I often tell audiences, "If you compete solely on price, proximity, or performance, you may as well give up." While proximity may matter to your current clients, trust me, it is not going to matter to your next generation of clients. Skype, Google Hangouts, and other "live" platforms have pushed the meaning of in-person meetings. Even physicians—people who typically provide face-to-face service—are able to "see" clients through online sources.

It is relatively simple to imagine the day when your clients won't care where you are located if you are someone who can answer their needs. Let's say, for example, you specialize in working with women in their fifties who've been so busy running a business and juggling parenting duties that they know they're way behind on their retirement. Those women—business owners who likely know what it means to serve customers around the globe—won't care where your office is if they feel a connection with you. They know what

---

2 "Winning Consensus-Based Sale," CEB, 2015, https://www.cebglobal.com/about.html.

it means to communicate using email, text, FaceTime, and so on. They're looking for someone who also knows how to operate in the digital space. (Example: One of my dear friends is a realtor. She recently closed on a property for one of her premier clients while on vacation in India! The initial inspection was done via Skype and a laptop camera.)

Managing Risk

Social media is altering the communication landscape. And while Lady Gaga, Justin Bieber, and Katy Perry are busy building their Twitter empires (with more followers than the entire populations of Germany, Turkey, South Africa, Canada, Argentina, United Kingdom, and Egypt!), they don't have the Financial Industry Regulatory Authority (FINRA), the US Securities and Exchange Commission (SEC), or other regulatory entities creating and overseeing rules for what they can and cannot do.

Granted, some advisors jump into the arena without a clear understanding of the requirements. But too many use compliance as an excuse not to participate. They avoid social media because they aren't willing to take the time to understand the regulations and outline a plan to be compliant. Know this: there are advisors participating—and succeeding.

There are many ways to manage a social media presence in a regulated environment while keeping risk to a minimum. While FINRA Regulatory Notices 10–06 and 11–39; the January 4, 2012, SEC Risk Alert; and a recent SEC alert regarding online-review sites address the rules you need to know, I'll make it all wonderfully simple.

First, a disclaimer: I am not an attorney, nor do I play one on TV. Second, I do not hold any licenses. (Wow, more than twenty-five years in the financial services space and I've managed to dodge that requirement.) With both of these caveats in mind, let me summarize the regulations:

- *What the rules require.* Interestingly, there are really no specific social media regulations. Nope. So far, the regulators have just applied existing regulations to social media. To summarize:

  □ Firms must adopt a social media policy that outlines how to interact with the world via social media. This policy must also outline how to train and monitor employees who are engaged in social media correspondence. Failing to enforce existing social- media policies, whether through record keeping or the storage of electronic communications, is the second-most common violation as reported by FINRA.[3]

  □ All communication via the Internet, including interaction on social sites, is the same as in-person or written communications.

---

3 Jason Wallace and Suzanne Barlyn, "Advisers Still Shaky on Social Media Policy," Reuters, May 30, 2012, accessed September 14, 2015, http://www.reuters.com/article/2012/05/30/net-us-socialmedia-exam-idUSBRE-84T0AQ20120530.

- □ Firms must retain and supervise social media activity and archive associated content for three years.[4]

- *Investment advice.* Making investment recommendations via social media is just messy. Don't do it. Social media is an avenue for broad distribution of content, and any advice will trigger the suitability requirements of FINRA Rule 2111. Watch out for any promissory language, unsubstantiated claims, and ratings.

- *LinkedIn traps.* Be mindful of recommendations or endorsements posted on your LinkedIn profile. They are considered to be testimonials, which are strictly prohibited. LinkedIn has an edit function that allows this area to be hidden. The SEC does accept endorsements that are not related to a professional's financial services. For example, endorsements for any volunteering work you do in the community may be displayed. However, the SEC will be on the lookout for comments that cross the fine line into your professional services.

- *Others' content.* Finally, there's third-party content. Social media is about sharing. In fact, posting only original content is actually a bit of a social media faux pas. In terms of regulations, sharing third-

---

4 "SEC Interpretation: Electronic Storage of Broker-Dealer Records," U.S. Securities and Exchange Commission, accessed September 14, 2015, http://www.sec.gov/rules/interp/34-47806.htm.

party content can be tricky. Financial advisors need to understand that they are held liable for the content they link to in their updates or posts.[5] Be aware that your firm will be held liable if you know or have reason to believe that the content you've shared contains false or misleading information. If nothing else, this makes sense from a reputation perspective. Who wants to be associated with misleading information anyway?

In short, electrons equal ink. Don't do anything on social media that you wouldn't do in real life. Whatever you choose to do online, be absolutely clear on your firm's policy, and work alongside the compliance folks if you have any nagging questions. For instance, the SEC is now allowing advisors to include links or logos to third-party review sites such as Yelp or Angie's List, and it is allowing firms to post these comments *directly* to your website. However, if you opt to post comments directly to your site, you must include any negative commentary along with all of the positive. Ah, the joys of contradiction!

Static Versus Interactive

Another piece of the social puzzle? Understanding the difference between static and interactive content.

---

5 "FINRA Rule 2210 Questions and Answers," FINRA, accessed September 14, 2015, http://www.finra.org/industry/finra-rule-2210-questions-and-answers.

Static content is associated with a specific social profile: your LinkedIn page, or your company's LinkedIn, Facebook, Twitter pages, and so on. Static content (including videos, articles, and samples posted to those profiles) requires preapproval, as does all advertising content.

Interactive content, such as LinkedIn posts, tweets, and Facebook updates, must be monitored and can be supervised after the fact. This type of interactive content must also be archived by your firm or a third party and retained for three years. It is likely that your firm already has an archiving solution. If not, third-party firms, such as RegEd, Smarsh, Erado, Socialware, Actiance, and so on, allow you to easily comply in much the same way your email is monitored.

I'll talk about blogs in detail later in the book. But for now, just know they may be considered static or interactive content. Check with your compliance officer for clarification.

Compliance Is Not an Excuse

Thankfully, rather than just saying no to social media, a growing number of organizations in the financial services world are easing up on some of their internal restrictions, giving advisors leeway to participate in the social sphere. Even if your social participation seems hindered by compliance, you have opportunities to create a personal brand and connect with your "tribe," which we'll talk about in the next chapter. You can still outconnect, outcare, and outsell your competition with a little effort.

Word of mouth is no longer the only tool you can rely on to build your business; you can begin to use "word of mouse!"

CHAPTER ONE ACTION STEPS

- Visit deconstructingdigital.com to download a copy of my "Seven Things to Know about Compliance."
- Visit deconstructingdigital.com to download a copy of my "Six Steps to a Spectacular Social Strategy."

CHAPTER TWO

Who's Your Tribe?

W ho is your ideal client? In his book *Tribes: We Need You to Lead Us*, best-selling author Seth Godin defines tribes as "any group of people, large or small, who are connected to one another, a leader, and an idea." I like his term, and I use it to describe an advisor's niche, or the ideal clients you want to attract.

But I go a step further with the message that advisors start feeling more responsible to their tribe online. Rather than just thinking of people as prospective clients, you should truly get into the heart and spirit of who your tribe members are and what you can do to *help* and support them. As an example, imagine if your tribe members were families who have children with special needs. Your expertise is focused on creating avenues to help them support their children in perpetuity. This clarity of focus will drive decisions around your services, your brand, your marketing—and even how you show up in the social space.

In thinking about my tribe, people and organizations in the financial services arena, I know that it's an extremely competitive world. The members of my tribe are juggling work, life, and family, not to mention navigating the regulatory issues, competition, and a surge in robo-advisors.

When I write content or think about my interactions online or on my blog, I make certain the information I provide is useful and speaks to my tribe. Before I begin typing, I conjure up an image of the individual(s) that I'm "speaking" with. Maybe it's an advisor just starting out. Or maybe an advisor in his midfifties who's not online, concerned that he's missing out.

Too often, when I ask about their ideal clients, advisors will answer, "anybody with money," or name groups such as small-business owners or women. The challenge with an extremely broadly based audience? You're destined to be a me-too, a generic advisor or a nearly faceless commodity.

According to CEG Worldwide, 70 percent of top financial advisors—those earning at least $1 million annually—focus on a particular niche.[6] The more willing you are to commit to a specific niche or tribe, the easier it will be to communicate with them, and the more meaningful your content and conversations.

Understandably, we all start our practices by serving everyone and anyone, which makes sense; we have to eat.

---

6 Jonathan Powell, "Pick Your Niche," CEG, http://www.cegworldwide.com/resources/expert-team/033-cwac-jon-powell-pick-your-niche.

But some advisors find it difficult to focus on a tribe because they're afraid of alienating other potential clients; a female advisor focused on the women's market may be afraid she's going to alienate her male clients. (In truth, she'll likely end up with more male clients in the form of her female clients' husbands, business colleagues, and family members.) There's obviously also the concern about alienating specific populations, particularly if you're in a smaller community where you appear to have a limited prospect base.

No matter where your tribe is, Florida or Fairbanks, if you provide enough value, you might end up having a national footprint for your solution. At the very least, you should be able to expand your region.

This focus, this tight niche, requires that you get gutsy. The word "no" must enter your vocabulary. For instance, I've turned down people from different industries who want my firm's help. "Not our area of expertise," I tell them. I've turned down firms who just want help with a singular piece of their marketing. I tell them we work with organizations that need a holistic approach. Staying uber focused on what we do frees me up to better serve my current tribe.

My challenge to you? Understand the segment you serve best, and target your marketing and social media presence accordingly. While you may like to think you serve everyone, there is a vast difference between the small-business client and the large corporation with stockholder scrutiny. Being all things to all people waters down your marketing message.

As an example, imagine if you only did financial plans for bike stores. (Granted, it would be a very small market, but you could own that market online—and off—in a very short period of time!)

Know, Like, Trust

Trust is a concerning issue in the financial services sector. The industry is challenged to overcome a bad reputation and to build credibility. Indeed, compared to other businesses and industries, financial services regularly comes in at the back of the pack. We have only a 51 percent trust rating compared to the tech sector, which garners a 74 percent trust rating, according to the Edelman Trust Barometer.[7]

People do business with people they know, like, and trust. Much of the knowing piece is really a two-way street: Do you know your audience/tribe members, and do they know you? The *like* and *trust* components, meanwhile, stem from the fact that we're influenced by people we like and respect.

The best way to begin to know your tribe members is to understand them. Step into their shoes by thinking about their persona: the way they talk and behave, the way they navigate the world, their worries and social drivers, and so on. Maybe begin with a list of your favorite clients. Why do

---

7 Edelman, "2016 Edelman Trust Barometer Global Results," accessed February 20, 2016, http://www.edelman.com/insights/intellectual-property/2016-edelman-trust-barometer/executive-summary/.

you enjoy working with them? Is it solely about profitability or revenue? Or is it a more personal or comfortable relationship? Then segment your full client base into three categories:

- revenue paid to your company annually—or possibly client profitability
- length of time in your relationship
- demonstrated willingness to be a reference

These criteria are practically perfect for highlighting the most profitable clients: those who stay with you the longest and say wonderful things about you and your firm.

Next, find the common characteristics of the clients on your list. Get super clear about the characteristics of your tribe. You might first think in terms of basic characteristics such as demographics (gender, age, income, occupation, education, etc.) and family stage (kids, ages, etc.). Perhaps, they work in the same industry, hold the same values for family and community, or possess a singular investment need or concern. You could also describe them by their psychographics, which include personality, lifestyle choices, and other criteria.

As you begin to imagine your ideal clients, take a deeper look and ask what their specific concerns or problems (pain points) are. By considering the following factors, you can uncover critical hot buttons and marketing opportunities to help guide your planning and marketing efforts:

- pressing financial concerns
- questions about financial future

- important financial or business goals
- specialized planning needs
- personal passions
- memberships
- hobbies or volunteer interests
- centers of influence

Finally, ask yourself how they like to communicate. You can communicate much more effectively if you can break your audience down into a couple of segments rather than just one. If you have C-suite groups, human-resources managers, and small-business owners to consider, look for common threads and issues. Likewise, your segments may prefer different communication vehicles; some may respond to emails, while others may prefer a quick phone call. And they will definitely use the social sphere in different ways.

The closer you can get to a detailed description of your tribe and the more specific you can be in understanding the characteristics and personal drivers of your niche, the easier it will be to create a marketing plan and associated content that stands out in a very noisy sales world.

Consistency Is Huge

On your way to work today, did you stop at Starbucks or Dunkin Donuts for your wake-up coffee? While waiting in line for that tall, skinny latte or straight-up Americano, did you consider why your coffee purveyor and other companies such as Disney, Apple, and Nike are so incredibly successful at establishing and keeping customer loyalty while others seem to shutter their doors only after a few months?

Consistency could very well be what drove you to your favorite coffee spot today. I know it works for me. When I head to Starbucks, I know my short flat white will be delectable and my dog, aBoo, will receive her consistently delicious "puppaccino"—a sizeable dollop of whipped cream in a cup.

All clients and customers love consistency. They enjoy knowing what to expect and come to expect what they know. The mega companies understand the power of consistency. They are diligent about their brand experience and work to have it permeate everything they do.

Several years ago, I had the opportunity to see Michael Eisner, former CEO of Disney, speak at a conference. In his speech, he metaphorically likened a consistent experience to a series of very small dots—somewhat like the art of pointillism—creating an overall image of the Disney organization.

Interestingly, a book written in 1984—*Influence: The Psychology of Persuasion* by Robert Cialdini—provides the perfect scientific foundation for the importance and validity of brand consistency. Cialdini confirms, scientifically, what Eisner knew intuitively: "A high degree of consistency is normally associated with personal intellectual strength," while someone whose actions are inconsistent is considered "indecisive, confused, two-faced, or worse." Consistency confirms to your clients and prospects that you're reliable, trustworthy, and possibly even smart!

A consistent digital-marketing effort will drive opportunities. If done well, over time, your tribe will begin to understand your voice, they'll start to see the value that you provide, and they will reward you with loyalty.

CHAPTER TWO ACTION STEPS

- Visit deconstructingdigital.com for "Your Tribe Online," an infographic to help you decide where to find your tribe online.

CHAPTER THREE

If Your Brand Were
a Superpower

In order to rule the digital realm, you must start with clear brand and brand purpose. Since the term brand purpose means nothing to most folks, consider this assignment as discovering your "superpower." Who is your village? What are you trying to save them from? And what is your superpower?

When you know your superpower, you know what you stand for and what you stand against. When you know your superpower, you are clear about how you help. When you know your superpower, you have a starting point for your marketing efforts.

For example, some folks talk at length about the fact that their superpower is their adherence to a fiduciary standard. Okay, that's fine. But does that adherence to a fiduciary standard mean anything to anybody? However, if your tribe members are millennials, and you therefore explain adherence to a fiduciary standard in terms of a force field (your super-power is that you provide a *force field* over someone's assets), then your tribe might understand your value a bit better.

While you may not wish to use superhero terms for your marketing, I am challenging you to think from a different perspective. All too often we use terms that make sense to us but that are not necessarily intuitive for our audience. And, all too often, we're saying the same thing over and over again.

Stop the Boredom

There's a shift happening in Western society, a shift away from a knowledge-based workforce toward one that sees patterns, creates stories, and combines unrelated ideas into something new. In his book *A Whole New Mind*, author Daniel Pink suggests the shift has been driven by abundance and the satu-ration of affordable products. In a nutshell, this saturation has accelerated many people's search for something beyond a commoditized life to a life that encompasses meaning, beauty, spirituality, and emotion.

This approach demands that you get out of your head and into your heart. (Likely a challenging thought in the business world!) Our hearts are where all fears and hopes and dreams come from, whether from a personal or a business perspective. We are emotional creatures. If your messaging is grounded from an emotional perspective—from the heart place—you will shift the perspective of your organization and your brand. You'll stand out from the multiples of boring and generic financial brands.

The consulting firm Walker, in its *Customers 2020* report, stated that price and product will soon be outflanked by customer experience as the key brand differentiator of the future.[8] Similarly, the firm calls upon organizations—and their workforces—to prepare for this change by including the story, meaning, and design behind their products or services and to consider all of these facets from the perspective of the customer experience.

Let's face it, financial services and banking can be considered quite boring and dry compared with Facebook and Google and fancy artistic bakeries. But why should we stay that way? We should and can push our organizations and our teams just a tad bit more toward the right side of our brains. Let's bring a bit more design, story, empathy, play, and meaning to our branding and client interactions.

Although the financial services marketplace is a highly regulated, highly logical subject, the truth is that financial decisions are wrapped up in people's upbringings. Our clients' earliest money stories are rooted in emotions. Those memories might be good and include some really amazing insights, or they might be filled with fear and doubt. Either way, they're usually extremely emotional because, ultimately, what we're talking about is someone's security. Think back to

---

8 Walker, Customers 2020, accessed September 15, 2015, http://www.walkerinfo.com/knowledge-center/webcasts/docs/Walker-Insights-Webcast-Customers-2020.pdf.

the Great Recession. Obviously, that was a difficult time; we all remember what a gut-drop that was. We saw anxiety and panic and fear—*emotions*. Or think about people who win the lottery. They don't sit right down and fill out a spreadsheet. The first thing they do is jump for joy—*emotions*.

Always Be Yourself, Unless You Can Be Batman—Then, Be Batman.

The problem? There's really only one Batman. When I review financial brands, I encounter a sea of sameness: images of compasses and bank columns and happy seniors dancing on the beach or golfing. Instead, I want you to take your business hat off and look at your consumer world and see what you appreciate about the businesses or brands that you engage with. Chances are when you walk into your coffee shop, you're greeted with a smile, not a check sheet.

Also note that your superpower can change over time. Your tribe of fifty-year-old, professional women may expand to include their network of colleagues and friends. The key is that you don't have to be perfect. Just pick something and do it. Chances are you're going to have to switch it around anyway.

Look at me: My first job in the financial services field was designing employee newsletters and brochures for 401(k) plans. Although I had a number of job opportunities at the time, I opted for the financial services firm, one that was at par with salary: no new car, no pay raise. My reason? I was a single mom, and I knew I needed to—no, I *had* to—learn more about money and finances in order to provide for my family.

What I learned because of my career in the financial services industry changed the trajectory of my life and my family's life. Now my purpose, my why, and my superpower is to change the world of financial services one word at a time.

Why change the world of finance one word at a time? The world of financial services is full of fear, shame, and doubt for many Americans. As I've mentioned earlier, to improve their world—and ours—we need to get out of our head and into our hearts. The words we write and speak are the starting point for this very important endeavor.

Be Passionate, Authentic, Transparent

What do you care about? That's what you talk about in the digital space. The more you can really identify what you care about, what you stand for, what your superpower is, the easier it's going to be for you to create content in this digital world.

Transparency, particularly in financial services, is something that's going to become more and more valued. Think about it: when you sit down with someone in your office, you're clear about who you are, what you stand for, and the value you bring to the table. Why should it be so difficult to be the same online?

If you say your superpower is to treat everything and everyone with dignity, that might influence where your organization donates money or where you choose to spend your time as a volunteer. That might also influence your decisions when you help clients invest their money. Maybe you'll naturally migrate to clients who choose to invest in socially responsible funds, as an example.

Now, some ideas, admittedly, aren't the best. There was a bank in Portland, Oregon, that tried to promote itself as a bank for dog owners—a fun idea but probably just a touch before its time. At the same time, there's a woman financial advisor in northern California whose dog is the mascot for her office. When people come to the office, they get the impression that the staff members there take care of everybody in their lives, even animals.

There's another advisor who feels strongly about the need for more diversity on boards in the United States. In fact, she has created a portfolio that evaluates whether an organization has three or more women on its board as a first screen. The clients that she works with feel strongly about the need for board diversity as well. And guess what? Her minimum client size is $5 million.

Don't Miss Out

Discovering your superpower and clarifying your brand is an important first step in the world of digital marketing. Unfortunately, many smaller or medium-size businesses get their logo and their letterhead and count that as brand development. But that's really not a brand.

Stand out and be different. Create a brand with meaning and heart. By standing out and being different, along with being extremely clear about your superpower, you'll create an extraordinary and differentiated brand experience. And here's the magic: a well-branded organization *increases the perceived value* of its services.

CHAPTER THREE ACTION STEPS

- Visit deconstructingdigital.com to download a copy of my "Discovering Your Superpower!"
- Visit deconstructingdigital.com to download a copy of my "Brand Touch Point Audit Checklist."

CHAPTER FOUR

Sharing Your Smarts

Historically, marketing has been about the many ways businesses can interrupt you: commercials, advertising, cold calls, billboards, and so on. You don't ask to be told about a local cancer treatment when you're driving to work, but that's what a billboard does. Most of these old-style, outbound, marketing efforts can be considered interruptions: a commercial in the middle of the newest *Walking Dead* episode; a subscription postcard placed inside a magazine; a robo-dialer telling you you've won that amazing vacation to Tahiti!

Thankfully, today we can avoid all those interruptions. We have DVRs that let us bypass commercials, we have the federal Do Not Call list, we can dump direct mail right into the recycle bin, and we can unsubscribe from, or block, bothersome email as spam.

However, there's another type of marketing known as inbound marketing, sometimes called content marketing, thought-leadership marketing, or as Seth Godin[9] coins it, permission marketing. Inbound marketing is an avenue for you to provide so much value to people that they will give you permission to market to them. Think of this approach as your "giving-your-smarts-away" strategy.

If you Google any subject, let's say, swimming pools, one (or more) of the responses to your query will likely be a white paper or some type of report on swimming pools. The company distributing that white paper is attempting to say, "You need help determining which swimming pool to buy. Let us be the one to help you." Ultimately, if you allow that pool company to send you all of its valuable information, to give you its smarts, then it might begin to nurture a relationship with you. And quite possibly, you may purchase your pool from the company.

In fact, for professional-services firms, this type of thought-leadership marketing is one of the more powerful ways to generate new business opportunities. Beginning in the 1960s when McKinsey & Company started publishing its *McKinsey Quarterly*, the firm has led the way in developing thought leadership as a business-development strategy.

The effectiveness of McKinsey's approach can be seen in how many other organizations have followed suit. In many

---

9 Can you tell I have a marketing crush on Seth Godin?!

ways, this launched the proliferation of white papers and reports that so many firms are producing today.

While generating original research or crafting white papers may not be your cup of tea, you can quickly differentiate yourself by finding a way to honestly, transparently, and authentically help people.

For example, if your tribe is families, maybe you'll create a series of six blog posts that provide step-by-step ideas and resources to help their kids plan to exit college debt-free. Some prospects will use the information and never call you. But others will realize that you know what you're talking about and reach out to you for more help.

If you continue to approach the social space from an avenue of giving, you're going to get your fair share over time.

What you're currently reading is one of my inbound marketing tools: I am giving my smarts away for a nominal fee, with the intention of eventually raising awareness of my capabilities with members of my tribe and as a result, growing my speaking and consulting business. And I'm extending the value of the book, giving away more of my smarts, through periodic invitations (calls to action) to go to my website and get a free download. While I'm building my credibility with the information I'm sharing, I also anticipate that some readers (or referrals) will likely engage my services.

The Essentials of Successful Sharing

To provide that "give," you need to consider three primary elements with your social media interaction: intention, story, and voice.

- *Intention.* Simply put: How are you helping people? As an advisor, there are countless ways you can provide valuable insight and understanding of what can be a confusing and complex undertaking. Social media postings allow you to give and, in turn, develop goodwill with your connections. With intentional, consistent, and meaningful postings, your social media interaction can help you build long-term relationships.

- *Story.* Your social media story should align with your brand and marketing message. In a sense, the story is your unique perspective—what you bring to the market that no one else can offer. To formulate your story, consider these questions:
  - ▫ What are your core values? (For instance, if you place emphasis on holistic financial services, you might want to share posts that address finances as they apply to varied aspects of living and learning, not just business services.)
  - ▫ What makes your firm truly different and unique?
  - ▫ What are you doing to make people happy?
  - ▫ What are you doing to inspire your community?

- *Voice.* Just as your intention and story need clarity and purpose, so does your voice. Be careful that you don't create a disconnect between who you are in person and who shows up on social media. Be true to yourself and your followers. If you are factual, funny, or friendly in person, be that way with your postings. Granted, you may tweak your voice a bit for different platforms, but the change shouldn't be too drastic. For instance, on LinkedIn, your updates should be a little more succinct and professional, while your Facebook posts can be more personal and relaxed.

Pay attention to word choice, sentence structure, and tone. Watch the use of jargon as well. If people expect industry-specific terminology, great, but if they don't, try to avoid it as much as possible. Infographics, photos, videos, and other visuals should also reflect your voice and personality.

Again, sometimes people feel they have to be very formal when they write, but online content must match offline voice. As far as I'm concerned, that makes things quite simple, in part because I have a touch of writing phobia. (I must have missed a grammar class in junior high.) When I try to sit down and write a formal white paper, I'm very challenged. However, when I sit down and write a blog post, I write as if I were speaking directly to a person. My word choice, my quirky approach to alliterations, my overabundance of commas—those things come through. The way I show up online through the written word sounds like me.

As for the "Trolls" . . .

One day, I sent out my weekly newsletter to my email list. It was a super helpful email about my favorite digital tools. Many people enjoyed it and even replied, asking whether the dog in the picture was a Newfoundland. However, one grumpy bunny was particularly awful. He used very bad words in his reply about the quality of my offering. I had two choices: I could celebrate that I had a 25 percent open rate or get down in the dumps because *one* person didn't appreciate what I had to say.

Here's the fact about creating content, being a thought leader, and giving your smarts away: there will be negative people. But think of it this way: you'd get zero responses if you were to do nothing. So I win. I'm doing something, I'm growing my influence, and I'm growing my business. I simply smile and count it as a win, snarky trolls and all. Don't fear the trolls. In truth, anyone can say negative things about you online, whether you're there to see them or not.

Whatever you do online, the key is to be as positive as you can. You don't want to bring people down by always drawing attention to the bad side of a situation. (People get enough bad news every day anyway.) Don't be a troll yourself, a mean-spirited person bent on tearing others down or sharing a gloomy worldview. That kind of attitude won't win you any points. In fact, it may just damage your personal/ professional brand.

CHAPTER FOUR ACTION STEPS

- Visit deconstructingdigital.com to download a copy of my "Thought Leadership Marketing Tips and Ideas."

CHAPTER FIVE
Your Digital Front Door

When I take my morning walk, I pass by an insurance agent's office, and peering through the windows, I can see a 1950s wooden desk, 1970s carpeting on the floor, and wood paneling on the walls. It's clean, but it's really old school, and I think *That's not the insurance person for me.* I make a judgment based on visuals, nothing else. If he were truly trying to pull off midcentury modern, there would be an obvious appeal. But that's not the case. He's in there every morning at six a.m., and I bet he works his tail off for clients, but I make an assumption based upon what his office looks like.

Our opinions of a company or a person are formed in that introductory split second. Research shows that our impression of a company's website is formed in less than one second.[10] That impression—positive or negative—shades

---

10 Gitte Lindgaard, Gary Fernandes, Cathy Dudek, and J. Brown, "Attention Web Designers: You have 50 milliseconds to make a good first impression!", vol. 25 of

our experiences and actions going forward. Unfortunately, that first assessment may be absolutely incorrect. But when we define these initial perceptions as fact, as seen through our (metaphorical) lens, they can be difficult to reframe. It's challenging to entertain alternate viewpoints. When our own prospects, clients, colleagues, or communities view us through a skewed lens, we may never have the opportunity to shift the perception of who we are and the value we bring.

Too often I see websites that were obviously put up years ago and then never updated, much like the insurance agent's office. Those websites are static, unresponsive, not mobile enabled—they're simply a revved-up brochure.

As the "digital front door" to your online presence, your website needs to be just as appealing as your physical office space. Just as you need to occasionally power-wash your office façade, you also need to keep up the entryway to your online presence.

Yes, it's human nature to judge based on appearance. And yes, your business is judged by the appearance of your website. Within fifty milliseconds—a blink of an eye—visitors will be able to form an opinion about your website. Just look at the numbers:

- According to research conducted by Stanford University, 75 percent of people judge a company's credibility based on its website.[11]

Behaviour & Information Technology (Taylor and Francis Group, 2006).
11 Nicole Denton, "10 Signs It's Time for a Website Facelift," HubSpot, March 10, 2014, accessed September 16, 2015, http://blog.hubspot.com/insiders/

- Ninety-four percent of respondents to a ResearchGate study say that they find websites with good design to be more trustworthy.[12]
- A 2012 study by FleishmanHillard found that the Internet had eclipsed the persuasive power of family, friends, or colleagues in influencing purchase decisions.[13] The study also found that 42 percent of people surveyed followed a brand on a social site, and 79 percent reported that they did so to learn about the brand.[14]

What does your website say about your business?

- poor or old design = outdated or mediocre
- last blog post was in 2014 = inconsistent or lazy
- slow or not responsive = technologically incompetent

Your website needs to be the hub of your entire digital-marketing ecosystem. It needs to be considered as a functioning member of the sales/marketing team. Beyond just presenting products and services, your website should also

should-i-redesign-my-website.

12 Ibid.

13 FleishmanHillard, "2012 Digital Influence Index Shows Internet as Leading Influence in Consumer Purchasing Choices," news release, January 31, 2012, http://fleishmanhillard.com/2012/01/news-and-opinions/2012-digital-influence-index-shows-internet-as-leading-influence-in-consumer-purchasing-choices/.

14 Ibid.

present some of your personality along with your deepest, richest, and best thought leadership: your blog posts will be there, as will your newsletter, news releases, and so on.

Your website provides you an avenue to be promotional. Being promotional in the social sphere is a no-no, but the content on your website will be preapproved. So this helps you get past the compliance issue as well. (You can have all the disclaimers and disclosures you need!)

Planning Your Website

A clean, easy-to-use design is a great start for a website, but it must also be focused. Before you get started, it's important to know the basic "W questions": Who am I marketing to? What am I offering? When is it time for people to use my services? Why am I a standout choice? And ultimately, where can I be reached?

As I mentioned earlier, I also like to pepper in the question, "What's my voice?" because that voice can be a valuable framing device that speaks to the visual aesthetic of your site and your service descriptions.

Remember that branding and design are key in every interaction, and the Internet provides a prime opportunity to make a dramatic and impressive impact. For instance, consider the retirement-plan experience in this context. By reviewing what happens when your prospects and clients interact with your firm to talk about retirement planning, you can identify simple, effective ways to enhance their overall experience. The confidence and ease gained during your clients' first impression will influence the way they view your services going forward. If they remember you were helpful and knowledgeable and you greeted them with a smile, they won't associate you and your business with the negativity of a stressful experience.

Your website also needs to send the right message. If you're telling your tribe that you're the most current, up-to-date advisor—you've got your finger on the pulse of the economy—then your website shouldn't feature that same, smiling, stock photo that also poses as a doctor or an attorney on other websites. And just as in the social space, your website voice needs to match your in-person voice. If you don't wear a suit and tie when you meet with your clients, but your website is very formal, that inconsistency is going to make people wonder what else is inconsistent.

If you look at my website, shoefitts.com, you'll see that it is professional, casual, and just a little bit quirky. That's because I'm not the marketing person for everyone. I want clients who are interested in pushing the boundaries of how we communicate in financial services. Just because I don't take myself too seriously doesn't mean I don't take my client relationships seriously. I absolutely do.

Website Checkup

When was the last time you lifted the hood on your website? Pretty pictures, a bio page, and a contact form alone won't cut it today. People use your web presence as an indicator of how effective you are in conducting business. Here are some of the basics you need to cover with your website. How does your website measure up?

- *Design and content.* Granted, pretty pictures alone will not do the trick, but your website does need to incorporate some basic design aesthetics to indicate you are a legitimate business. Your value proposition—or superpower—should be very clear so visitors know what you do, how this helps them, and why you do what you do. Include information on your services and key staff members. Tell your readers how your products and people meet their needs (not yours). While this content may not change frequently, you should review it at least once a year to make any necessary updates—and more often if you have key personnel, service, or product changes.

- *Jargon overload.* I mentioned this as part of your social-realm writing, but here again, speak to your audience in plain, simple English. When you go to your attorney, you don't need her to tell you that you've established *res ipsa loquitor.* You just want to know that she can fix your problem. Your clients feel the same way.

- *Saying the same ol' thing.* How many financial sites read some version of "We offer a wide range of fully customizable options to meet the needs of today's changing retirement environment"? Yep, almost all of them. You can fix this by doing your homework and reviewing competitors' websites. Look at how they position themselves, and then find your niche. Perhaps, it's by customer type or investment philosophy or product mix. Whatever it is, show your prospects that you are different, that you're not one of the crowd.

- *Navigation.* The most important rule in developing navigation is to not make the user think at all. Label your menus from the users' standpoint. Nobody knows what a tab labeled "Academic Rigor" means. Ask a teen or young adult to find your investment philosophy on your site. If they can't do it lickety split, fix it so they can.

- *Current thought leadership.* As I mentioned earlier, your website will house your blogs and articles demonstrating your thought leadership. Show everyone you have the pulse of the industry by keeping this information timely.

- *Social engagement.* When you publish an article on your website and do nothing else, you are "pushing" content. Today we have to "pull" our users to us, and social media is the way to do that; your e-newsletters and social media posts will drive people to your website so they can read your newsworthy and compelling blogs and articles. If customers become your friends on Facebook or follow you on Twitter, every time you post an article or tell them about a conference you're attending and what you're learning, your credibility goes up one tick at a time. Let's start ticking.

- *Social media icons.* Conversely, you must also include links on your website to your activities on social media. Wherever you are—LinkedIn, Twitter, Facebook, and so on—include an icon linking to each platform. There is no need to have these on the top portion of your site, as it's best to keep them on your website longer, rather than bouncing off to Facebook.

- *E-newsletter subscription.* Similarly, you should provide a separate widget so visitors can subscribe to your monthly e-newsletter. This gives you another permission-based marketing tool and lead generator.

- *Search engine optimization (SEO).* Include keywords in your content and on your website to raise your Google appeal. However, don't just throw around a bunch of "in" words without providing the content to back up those topics (this is known as keyword stuffing).

- *Contact information.* Make it easy for people to find the best avenue to contact you.

One last piece of the puzzle (a biggie): According to the Pew Research Center, nearly two-thirds of Americans (64 percent) own a smartphone. This is almost double the number of users (35 percent) in 2011.[15] In April 2015, Google changed its algorithm, and now, in order to appear appropriately in Google mobile searches, websites must be mobile enabled.

Your website is a crucial part of your business- and relationship-development efforts. Keep it relevant, up to date, mobile enabled, and an ongoing reflection of you and your firm.

Now let's look at some of the other gear in your marketing toolkit. We'll start with a standard tool that's actually had remarkable staying power—email.

CHAPTER FIVE ACTION STEPS

- Visit deconstructingdigital.com for a copy of my "10 Best Practices for Websites."

---

15 Aaron Smith, "U.S. Smartphone Use in 2015," Pew Research Center, April 1, 2015, accessed September 16, 2015, http://www.pewinternet.org/2015/04/01/us-smartphone-use-in-2015/.

CHAPTER SIX
Email: A Marketing Must-Have

P icture yourself in line at a busy grocery store, with two people are in front of you. What are you likely to do to kill time? Rather than paging through the *National Enquirer*, chances are you're going to use your smartphone to catch up on email.

Email readership is increasing, in part because now people can carry their inbox around with them. And also because poor or useless content is automatically routed to your spam folder. In fact, according to Smart Insights, email was the top-rated digital channel in 2015 for improving customer communications and loyalty.[16]

Today's email marketing is about providing a little touch point of value for your clients and prospects. It's a prime opportunity for you to give your smarts away and lead people back to your website. My email newsletters contain short, actionable notes that the reader can do, whether they contact me or not.

---

16 Susanne Colwyn, "State of the Art Digital Marketing 2015," Smart Insights, accessed September 16, 2015, http://www.smartinsights.com/managing-digital-marketing/marketing-innovation/state-of-digital-marketing/attachment/stateoftheartdigitalmarketingsmartinsights/.

Despite the popularity and onslaught of email, it remains one of the best ways to nurture leads. According to a Marketing Sherpa Email Marketing Benchmark Survey, a mighty 60 percent of marketers believe that email marketing produces return on investment. Around the same time, eMarketer released its *Email Marketing Benchmarks: Key Data, Trends and Metrics* report, in which it predicts the continued steady growth of email through 2016: "For marketers trying to reach consumers, email remains one of the best ways to find them."[17]

Breaking through the Noise

For financial advisors, email marketing is a must-have. Why? As a small- to medium-size firm, you are up against established players that have deeper resources, better brands, and more customers, day after day. It is the story of David versus Goliath, the famed parable about how an underdog defeated a giant in the days when the accepted approach to fighting was to don armor and swing swords. David, the underdog, shed his armor because it was too heavy. And because he had no skill with swords, he used a slingshot to defeat his foe, the giant.

Admittedly, it's a story that makes entrepreneurship exciting! So the question is: How do you beat your Goliath?

---

17 "Email Marketing Benchmarks: Key Data, Trends and Metrics," eMarketer, February 2013, accessed September 21, 2015, http://www.emarketer.com/public_media/docs/eMarketer_Email_Marketing_Benchmarks_Key_Data_Trends_Metrics.pdf.

How do you become nimbler, break through the noise, and garner the attention of your tribe? Well, one small shift can make a big difference in your sales and marketing efforts. While closing the deal is top priority, keeping leads coming in the door is what allows sales to get to the point of close. That is where lead nurturing comes in—and where email comes in.

Relationship building is a prime purpose of email marketing. With an email program in place, you can focus your in-person attention on your hot prospects and nurture the not-ready-yet prospects with a light touch. Email also lets you keep your brand and expertise at the forefront where prospects can easily access it. You know the term "top-of-mind"? I prefer the "be unforgettable" approach. My job as a businessperson is to be unforgettable. Outbound emails—helpful email—allow me to stay in touch and eliminate the need to contact every lower-level lead on a monthly basis.

Early on, email newsletters were simply online versions of the more conventional printed newsletters: four pages with fancy headers and six articles with pictures. However, the world of online content and news has shifted our expectations of the newsletter. Best practices reveal that shorter, bite-size content is the most well received—and the most read. In fact, most people read your newsletter on their smartphones! *More email is read on mobile devices than on desktops.*[18] Steer clear

---

18 Jordie van Rijn, "The Ultimate Mobile Email Stats Overview," accessed February 17, 2016, http://www.emailmonday.com/mobile-email-usage-statistics.

of loading your readers down with multiple articles. Chances are your newsletter could end up in the delete folder.

This is great news: the shorter your content, the better. And thanks to a variety of simple email creation platforms such as MailChimp, Constant Contact, Emma, and more, you don't have to be a fancy web designer.

The biggest pushback I get about email is from people telling me that no one reads them anyway. To which I reply that I don't care. Let's say I've got a mailing list of two hundred or two thousand or two hundred thousand. If 16 percent of my mailing list, which is the average for professional services,[19] voluntarily chooses to engage with my content, I'd be all over that every day. Sixteen percent of two hundred contacts is thirty-two people. Wouldn't you want to talk to thirty-two contacts every day if you could?

At ShoeFitts Marketing, our newsletter open rates range from 14 to 25 percent. This means that each time we send a newsletter, we have the chance for one in four people on our list to read our content. That is fantastic! Obviously, this means that three out of four recipients don't open. However, they do see the subject line and they do see the sender, a brand touch point that allows me to sneak in a tiny whisper about our expertise.

---

19 "Frequently Asked Questions," Constant Contact, accessed February 17, 2016, http://support2.constantcontact.com/articles/FAQ/2499#Comparison.

A Penguin, Panda, and Hummingbird Walk into a Bar

Let's back up and discuss an important component of your digital outreach: blogging. The root of the term *blog* came from Weblogs, a place where people—even those without any technical or coding expertise—published original content. This allowed people across the world the power to share their perspectives and ideas. Add in the capacity for interaction and commenting, and writers had a direct relationship with the reader.

Blogs can provide insight and commentary on a particular subject or can simply be an online diary. They vary in length from one sentence to seven hundred words or more and, typically, include additional links to other blogs, resources, and websites. At minimum, blogging once each month provides several important components for your digital strategy:

- *Google.* Google's search algorithms with code names such as Penguin, Panda, and Hummingbird are programs developed with the purpose of outwitting tricksters using black hat search engine optimization (SEO) efforts to grab higher website rankings. (Black hat techniques are "deliberate manipulation of search engine indexes."[20] They can

---

20 Wikipedia, "Spamdexing," accessed February 17, 2016, https://en.wikipedia.org/wiki/Spamdexing.

include participating in link farms or overstuffing keywords.)

Penguin, Panda, and Hummingbird algorithms review a website's inbound links, structure, and content on an ongoing basis. While paying an expert for SEO services may fit into your organization's marketing tactics, one of the first and best ways to bump your SEO is content, content, content. In fact, professional SEO firms often create content or ask that you create content as a first step in the search-engine optimization process.

- *Website visitors.* Quite a bit of business opportunity in our world of financial services arrives at your doorstep via a referral. So, while folks aren't blindly searching for "financial advisors Cincinnati," as an example, many will do their homework prior to meeting with you. This homework will likely begin via Google and end on your website.

  An ongoing effort for relevant and timely content will solidify your expertise in the minds of your visitors. Note this: if the last newsletter article or blog on your site is outdated or has moss growing on it, it can similarly damage their perception of you.

- *E-newsletter or email content.* There are a couple of ways to do e-newsletters, and which is best really depends on a bit of testing with your readers. One option is to list a few highlights from your blogs in your email, and then, with each highlight, link readers back to your site to read the full story. If your audience is more likely to read via smartphone, include the full article in the email itself so they can pull it up, read the article, and move on. Yes, you read that right! Use the same content in an outbound email that you place on your website. Most folks aren't subscribing to blogs these days. Rather, "blog" content is being proactively emailed to subscribers instead.

- *Format.* There are several schools of thought on the best format. One option is to use the fewest graphics possible: no masthead, no pictures. This makes your readers feel that you personally sat down and jotted a helpful note to them. Limiting graphics or images also reduces the need for a graphics person to be involved with each broadcast you send. And, given the different email platforms, limiting graphics may help with deliverability.

Getting Started

When I first began writing and creating content, I had a bit of trepidation. I'm not an English major, nor did I pass grammar with flying colors. And I hadn't written in quite some time. (Wow—really, since college.) My business reputation was on the line. I needed to ensure my content added to people's perception of my expertise. (That's the point. Right?) The best thing I did was hire a professional editor to review and edit my drafts for me. This helped in two ways. First, I could be confident that the final product was of professional quality. Second, I found that writing became easier. Knowing I had an editor to review my content, I didn't have to listen to the critical, English-teacher voice while creating content. I could simply write.

My other concern was what to write about. I was afraid I would run out of ideas. Interestingly, the more you write, the more you begin to realize that content is everywhere. Everyday activities can bring to mind analogies with financial topics. For instance, the decisions that people make at the grocery store about buying or not buying organic food could, perhaps, be equated to value investing. Or the decision you make regarding what the tooth fairy pays at your house may be a launching pad for a discussion about kids and money. You'll soon realize that writing is a muscle. The more you use it, the better you become. And the more you write, the more fun it becomes!

For now, if you're having trouble getting started, write about something you've read. Or think about some of the questions people ask you—or don't ask you—such as:

- What are the benefits and drawbacks of combining all my 401(k) plans into one?
- What do I do about planning for increased health-care costs?

- How do I decide on the best financial advisor?
- What can I teach my kids about saving that I never learned?
- Is my child too old for a 529 plan?
- How much is too much to pay in advisor fees?

As for length, brevity is just fine. Most people have limited time and a limited attention span. (And you likely don't have time to create a one-thousand-word essay anyway. Save your longer posts for valuable e-books and such. We'll talk about those later.) You can share your smarts and give real value in 350 to 500 words max. Even one article of around 250 words can express what you need your tribe to know.

Know this: headlines really matter. Your blog article and any email you send must have a good headline or subject line. If you're concerned that no one is reading your newsletter, it might be because your subject line—simply put—sucks. Are you particularly interested in the subject line "Fourth Quarter Newsletter"? Likely not. However, if your clients are very interested in how the economy is doing, or they're highly competitive and very focused on their returns, instead of "Fourth Quarter Newsletter," a more appealing subject line might be, "A Microcosm of Brazil and Its Impact on Emerging Market Funds." (Although, that sounds particularly heavy to me.)

A very popular and easy approach for content is "listicles," in which articles are structured around lists. "Five Ways to Harness a Down Market for Your Portfolio," or

"Seven Must-Knows about Medicare," or "Ten Little-Known Facts about the Economy." Listicles are everywhere because they tend to have a higher readership.

As for frequency, one of my colleagues sends out something every Tuesday, whether it is a quote or a thought or a picture with a couple of sentences. For many people, keeping up with a weekly newsletter is very challenging; I recommend a minimum of once a month.

CHAPTER SIX ACTION STEPS

- Visit deconstructingdigital.com for a copy of my "100 Tips for Social Media Success."

CHAPTER SEVEN
LinkedIn: The World's Rolodex

Imagine having access to nearly four hundred million professionals worldwide. Even better, imagine knowing how you might be connected to them via a client, center of influence, colleague, or friend. Exploring these connections feels a bit like the parlor game Six Degrees of Kevin Bacon. The game sought to find how Kevin Bacon was connected to other Hollywood insiders in fewer than six degrees. (It's from the concept of six degrees of separation explored way back in 1929 by Frigyes Karinthy.) In a sales and marketing environment, you're well aware that introductions and connections open doors more easily.

Today, LinkedIn operates the world's largest professional network on the Internet, with nearly four hundred million members in more than two hundred countries and territories. More than 110 million professionals are located in the United States. LinkedIn continues to grow at a rate of more than two new members *per second*.[21] LinkedIn's goal for total membership? Three billion!

Indeed, LinkedIn is the world's largest Rolodex. Reid Hoffman started LinkedIn out of a desire to build and

---

21 "About Us," LinkedIn, https://press.linkedin.com/about-linkedin.

leverage networks. "I realized that the world was transforming every individual into a small business," he told a reporter. "But how do you positively influence your brand on the net? How do you assemble a team fast? Who has the expertise to guide you? The power of the Internet is to accelerate the way you do business. I was very interested in this whole notion of each of us as individual professionals who are on the Internet and how that changes the way we do business, our careers, our brand identity."[22]

LinkedIn was also the first social platform that many broker-dealers approved. According to Emily Friedman of LinkedIn and Neil Benedict of FTI Consulting, who put together the white paper "Financial Advisors' Use of Social Media Moves from Early Adoption to Mainstream:"

> Traditionally, financial advisors depend on referral networks and cold calling to gain new clients; they also rely on frequent interactions with existing clients to deepen current relationships. Especially for newer advisors, it often can take years to build an effective network. By leveraging LinkedIn, advisors can streamline and amplify these efforts, using a single platform both to gain new clients and to deepen existing relationships.[23]

---

22 Reid Hoffman, interviewed by Mark Lacter, "How I Did It: Reid Hoffman of LinkedIn," *Inc.* magazine, May 1, 2009, http://www.inc.com/magazine/20090501/how-i-did-it-reid-hoffman-of-linkedin.html.

23 Emily Friedman and Neil Benedict, Financial Advisors' Use of Social Media Moves from Early Adoption to Mainstream, May 2012, accessed September 10, 2015, https://business.linkedin.com/content/dam/business/marketing-solutions/global/en_US/site/pdf/wp/linkedin-research-financial-advisors-use-social media.pdf.

Put differently, dialing for dollars is just no way to drum up business; cold calling is dead. Not to mention that cold calling is one to one. Meanwhile, focused, digital outreach allows you to immediately scale your networking efforts. Now you're able to connect one to many.

Here's how easy (and great) LinkedIn is: in the time it took me to type out the first couple of paragraphs of this chapter, I was able to also post something to LinkedIn. With that single post, I have the potential to reach nearly five thousand people currently in my LinkedIn network, a number of people I certainly could not manage in one week of phone calls, let alone a month!

And as many financial advisors eventually discover, LinkedIn provides access to an educated, financially savvy clientele, including a whopping 49 percent of American adults who gross more than $100,000 annually. [24]

As a trusted business-to-business resource, LinkedIn allows you to deepen your current relationships by discovering more about your clients, their background, and their connections. In addition, LinkedIn allows you to peek into your best clients' Rolodex and search for connections and prospects. The advanced search function allows you to segment and search for your specific prospects.

---

24 Neil Vidyarthi, "SURVEY: 49% of LinkedIn Users Have Household Income Over $100K," January 9, 2012, http://www.adweek.com/socialtimes/survey-49-of-linkedin-users-have-household-income-over-100k/88454.

How It Works: A Primer

Imagine being in the middle of a very crowded room at a conference or networking event. Working the room, you introduce yourself, introduce others, and likely exchange business cards.

That is how it works on LinkedIn. After you create and optimize a professional profile, you connect with others by, essentially, exchanging digital business cards—and a touch more. And now, rather than having a huge wad of cards in your pocket and wondering how in the world you're going to follow up with everyone (only to find out one or two of them are actually viable prospects), you have a simple and scalable way to stay in touch and share ongoing, valuable information. As LinkedIn continues to build out the CRM (client relationship management) and Sales Navigator functions of the platform, this may get easier and easier.

You've likely noticed when you Google individuals' names, their LinkedIn profile is consistently on the first page of search results. That's because LinkedIn is extremely Googlicious, meaning it assists in helping you rank higher in a Google search.

Are you clear on what folks see when they Google you? Imagine when people search for you or your business. Given the Googliciousness of LinkedIn, chances are they'll find your LinkedIn profile. Their first impression may even be formed by your LinkedIn profile photo.

The secret to tapping into this Googliciousness is an optimized LinkedIn profile. Here's a quick overview of the critical components of a LinkedIn profile to get you started. (By the way, making changes to your profile via the LinkedIn app on your mobile device isn't my cup of tea. Use LinkedIn via your desktop. It is faster, easier, and helps you avoid the regularly shifting interface.)

Profile Photo

A foundational element of a good LinkedIn profile is a professional headshot, an image that matches how you'll look when visiting with a prospect for the first time. Be professional and authentic: no pictures from weddings, no pictures with others cropped out, no dogs (unless you're a dog trainer).

Set aside your excuse about not being a model or a famous celebrity, or possibly, a concern for privacy. You must have a professional headshot for your profile. It's your first chance to communicate that you are friendly, professional, and trustworthy, and it attributes crucially in getting people to engage with you. Not convinced? Here are a few more compelling reasons:

- *Visibility.* LinkedIn's research shows that simply including a picture makes your profile fourteen times more likely to be viewed by others.[25]

25 Lydia Abbot, "5 Tips for Picking the Right LinkedIn Profile Picture," LinkedIn, December 31, 2014, https://business.linkedin.com/talent-solutions/

- *Credibility.* By hiding behind the default gray head, you limit your ability to create any type of professional impression. A missing photo will likely prompt viewers to question your lack of a picture. When you're at a networking meeting, do you hide behind the curtains and hope someone will do business with you?

- *Personal appeal.* You're in the business of helping people. Your identity, your eyes, your smile, your face—your photo—is a critical step toward building a compelling personal brand. The best way to ensure the highest-quality photo? Have a professional photographer take your headshot. Yes. That is an investment. However, don't let the price tag cloud your vision of the precious value of first impressions. A professional photographer will make certain you are comfortable, the lighting is perfect, the background is free from distractions, and possibly, even add in a little bit of Photoshop touch-up here and there. In most cases, the photographer may even allow a wardrobe change to increase your options.

Summary

All too often the Summary section on LinkedIn is either blank or not fully developed. People do business with people

blog/2014/12/5-tips-for-picking-the-right-linkedin-profile-picture.

they know, like, and trust. And your summary is the exact place to begin that journey. Help people get to know you, not your resume.

- *Tell your story.* Think back to the discussion about exploring your superpower and articulating your why. Why do you do what you do? What are you passionate about? How do you help people?

- *A blank summary is a missed opportunity.* Your summary is the first thing a prospect or connection sees in your experience section. If you don't create one, your profile will read like a resume. Yawn. How will your prospects and connections learn about you beyond your job history?

- *LinkedIn is a search engine.* Pay attention to the words and phrases you use as you construct your summary. You've got about two thousand characters to write about yourself. Use keywords that appeal to your potential prospect's needs and wants. If you're a Premium member, LinkedIn will offer suggestions of additional keywords to add and highlight strong business words that you're already using in your content.

- *A simple formula.* Consider the following as a helpful outline to start:
  - Who are you?
  - What's your why?
  - Where or how did you get your start?

- What are you passionate about with respect to your advisory work?
- What about your family or community?
- How do you spend your free time?
- What is your list of specialties? (This provides a great way to load up on meaningful keywords.)
- What is your call to action?

- Don't just tell; show. Finally, do you have a short introductory video you could include? Any white papers or presentations that folks may find exceptionally helpful? You can add those as a part of your summary as well.

Experience

Are you looking for a job? Or are you looking to build connections that benefit your business? Those are the questions you must ask yourself as you build out the Experience area. When LinkedIn began, the company suggested that folks cut and paste content from their resume. Times have changed.

Consider this: How authoritative does your LinkedIn profile read if it lists that you stay within a product budget, exceed at managing people, or provide strategic leadership? Those are the buzzwords of a job hunter.

If you're seeking to grow your sales and deepen relationships, use your experience area to show how you *help* your clients. Include words that show your expertise and your commitment to the market you serve. Whatever you do, don't leave the description blank. Once again, you'd waste valuable space that could be used to benefit your efforts.

How far back should your experience listing go? That's a tough one. The best answer? Until you feel as if you've listed the necessary positions to prove your expertise. If you're new to financial services, don't be concerned about listing previous positions. Every step of your life can point to how you've landed in the world of helping people navigate complicated investments, financial planning, risk management, and retirement issues.

Growing Your Network

First, let's talk about numbers. Have you ever been to a restaurant that is mostly or completely empty? It could seem pleasant enough, but the moment you arrive, doubts creep in: Why isn't anyone here? Is the food horrible? Granted, it is challenging when the reverse is true and you have to wait forty-five minutes for a table, but in that situation, doubts about the food never come up. The people inside are enough. They're providing social validation or social proof.

When it comes to establishing social proof, consider this fact: people with five hundred-plus connections on LinkedIn appear connected and credible, even if most of their connections are with partial strangers. Whom would you be more likely to trust, a person with seventy connections or one with over five hundred?

More connections also means a higher chance of being seen. More and more business leaders are joining LinkedIn and, whether you're looking for new clients or connecting with centers of influence, this site is a great place to be found.

Remember that LinkedIn is a search engine. The more optimized your profile and the more connections you have, the better you appear in your prospects' search results.

Also if you have something to say or just want to speak your mind in a professional manner, LinkedIn presents an *excellent* opportunity to get your voice heard. A higher connection count can lead to your profile reaching a larger audience. The larger your network, the more people you can influence. Put another way—bigger net, more fish.

One caveat: I'm not a fan of network stuffing—connecting with people just to grow your network numbers. I'm about quality. Remember, you are judged by the company you keep.

Here are some tips for growing your online network:

- *Remember that manners matter.* If you're reaching out to connect with someone, include a personal note in your request. The hollow and generic request on LinkedIn is just that—hollow and generic. It doesn't provide any context, personal or otherwise, about why you're interested in connecting.

- *Your friends are a reflection of you.* If you're ever concerned about a connection request, simply decline. If people don't know you, they aren't likely to be offended. If you feel compelled to respond, simply reply (without accepting) and ask them to share a bit more about their request and why they think connecting would be a good idea.

- *Say thank you.* Finally, always say please and thank you. When someone sends you a connection request and you accept, quickly send a thank-you note. It helps solidify the relationship. In many cases, I use this as an opportunity to invite my new connections to subscribe to my newsletter or podcast.

- *Be active and proactive.* LinkedIn allows you to digitally share articles and ideas you've read with a single individual or your whole network. With each meaningful post, you've garnered just a tiny bit more mindshare. Commenting on other people's postings is also beneficial; those small impressions can grow over time and create opportunities and relationships.

- *You can always leave.* Thankfully, you can always remove a connection after you've accepted it. Simply look for the blue rectangular box to the lower right of a person's profile photo. Use the drop-down menu and select "remove connection." And no, that person won't get a big red notice with this action.

As a cybersleuthing tool, LinkedIn is invaluable. The Advanced Search function allows you to search the largest database of professionals in the world (even without the paid subscription). Before picking up the phone, sending an email, or stepping out the door to your next meeting, spend fifteen minutes to review an individual's LinkedIn profile. Start by scanning the profile to gather insight on background, interests, and career path. Then take a few minutes more to review the following:

- *Summary.* Many folks use their bio as a summary. But the summary may also reveal an interesting tidbit about an individual's family, community, or extracurricular activities. (A connection of mine even lists being a vegetarian.)

- *Experience.* Has the individual been with one organization for twenty-plus years? If so, what does that say about that person's preference for consistency, loyalty, or possible aversion to risk? Is there any employer background about charitable activities, regulatory or legal trouble, or any recent leadership changes?

- *Recent activity.* Near the bottom right of a profile picture is the magic blue rectangle box with a drop-down arrow. Select the "View Recent Activity" option to see any recent updates or posts the individual may have written or shared. Another helpful drop-down option is the ability to save information to PDF, which is a handy way to create a document for offline reading or filing.

- *Group membership.* LinkedIn Groups can provide ways to connect with, and learn about, your prospects and clients. If the groups listed on individuals' profiles show they are members of an alumni group or group connected to their industry, you can use their participation as an insight into their interests or professional motivations.

- *Volunteer and causes.* Individuals may list a variety of volunteer positions and causes they participate in or donate to.

- *Influencers.* LinkedIn Influencers are an exclusive group of industry experts handpicked to become leading voices on the platform. Which Influencers do your prospects follow? Which major topics do they follow? There are many national and international thought leaders contributing content on LinkedIn.

- *Companies.* Just as folks may follow LinkedIn Influencers, they may also follow a variety of companies. These may be previous or current employers, firms that interest them from a business perspective, or the firms where their partners/ spouses work.

By researching and considering what is important, meaningful, valuable, and helpful for your prospects and clients, you'll be prepared with appropriate resources and helpful ideas regarding issues they may be facing in their financial world.

LinkedIn is a great way to dip your toe into the social space. It's easy to set up, easy to maintain, and it moves at a comfortable pace, although it's exponentially speeding up these days. Even if you choose not to do all the updates and engagement and all of that "rah rah, sis boom bah stuff," you can still use LinkedIn as a Rolodex on steroids.

CHAPTER SEVEN ACTION STEPS

- Visit deconstructingdigital.com to download my "LinkedIn Profile Optimization Guide."
- Visit deconstructingdigital.com to download my "Seven Ways to Show Up Prepared."

CHAPTER EIGHT

Trending on Twitter

R emember when twitter meant a bird's song, and a # was better known as a pound symbol? Today, Twitter conjures up a blue bird company logo and a worldwide social-networking platform, allowing users the ability to send and read 140-character messages called tweets. Twitter now boasts over 320 million active users who post five hundred million tweets per day and around two hundred billion tweets per year. No wonder it moves so quickly. That nets out to about six thousand tweets per second![26]

Getting started with Twitter is a bit like walking into the Mall of America—so many options, so many stores, and so much noise. There is an endless supply of people to follow, influential bloggers to read, news to discover, and a rabbit hole or two to explore. For some, the thought of using Twitter feels somewhat like whack-a-mole: full of chaos and noise.

Before you dive in, know this: your Twitter profile will appear in search engine lists—much as your LinkedIn profile

---

26 "Twitter Usage Statistics," Internet Live Stats, http://www.internetlivestats.com/twitter-statistics/.

does—if folks are looking for your name. So, as with all social platforms, a half-baked effort can impact your reputation and your personal brand. First, evaluate whether your target market is on Twitter and then consider whether you have the time for participation.

Pew Research regularly publishes statistics regarding usage of social platforms. For Twitter, it cites that some 23 percent of all online adults use Twitter. These users tend to be younger (under fifty years old) and urban.[27]

Much as TV allows you to watch specific shows, Twitter allows you to follow particular individuals and companies without the need for their permission or acceptance. It's somewhat like being an audience member with the option to interact with fellow audience members and the speaker.

LinkedIn requires that all profiles be that of an individual (though that individual has the option to create a company page). The platform on Twitter allows the profile to be that of an individual, organization, avatar—or even a snake, such as the Bronx Zoo's cobra! Most big brands—Heinz Ketchup, Alaska Airlines, Tide detergent—tweet as an entity. The decision you'll face is whether to present yourself as an individual or present your business entity. There are positives for either approach. However, I tend to lean toward creating an individual profile. (People do business with people. They opt

---

27 Maeve Duggan, "The Demographics of Social Media Users," Pew Research Center, August 19, 2015, http://www.pewinternet.org/2015/08/19/the-demographics-of-social media-users/.

to work with you because they know, like, and trust you. Yes. I know I am repeating myself.)

Remember the magic of digital marketing is content, contact, and consistency. So, as with any of the platforms in the wired world, you need an overarching plan and strategy with Twitter. For instance, do you have a stated purpose, a definition of success, and a way to measure your efforts? Here are some strategies Twitter is good for:

- expanding and interacting with your client base
- pointing people to your website
- sharing your smarts to build customer trust and loyalty
- promoting a special event
- eliciting a call to action

Likewise, your plan may define your success on Twitter in multiple ways by considering increases in your number of followers, readers of your tweets, people who want to retweet and/or carry on a conversation you initiate, and click-through rates to your website or your call to action. Twitter has dashboards that let you measure these results. They include the followers dashboard, which offers a quick breakdown of interests, location, gender, and the viewer's followers. Then there is the audience-insights dashboard, which lets you also see audience percentages by language, lifestyle types, buying style, household income, net worth, occupation, wireless carrier, education, and marital status. There is also a comparison feature that lets you see your audience insights against all Twitter users.

In addition, your tweet activity page shows you a breakdown of your tweets, retweets, replies, and promotions by impressions (number of times users saw the tweet); engagements (clicks on the tweets, retweets, replies, follows, and favorites); and engagement rate (engagements divided by the number of impressions).

A World of Hashtags

Ahh . . . hashtags. By now you probably have some idea of what these are about, or at least you've been seeing them everywhere. But let me explain.

Twitter uses hashtags (also known as the pound symbol, #) to group digital matter with other related, online content. The hashtag precedes a keyword or phrase about your subject matter. Hashtags increase the visibility of your posts and improve your chances of more views. For example, when media outlets streamed content related to the government shutdown to various social media platforms, they commonly used the hashtag #shutdown in related posts. This collective tagging effort neatly organized all related content so interested parties could find everything they wanted to see in one central location.

Used first on Twitter in the mid-2000s, hashtag capabilities exist today on most mainstream channels of social media including Twitter, Facebook, Pinterest, and Instagram.

While many businesses were, initially, slow to embrace them, hashtags are now an integral part of nearly all business-to-business and business-to-consumer marketing and communication vehicles. (Note that I did not include LinkedIn.)

Here are some tips for using hashtags:

- *Be relevant.* Just as we Google the web using keywords and phrases, social media users look up information by pairing a hashtag symbol and a topic (for example, #wealth or #financialliteracy). Don't tag "article" words such as #a or #an. And don't include hashtags just to draw attention to yourself. If your content is not applicable, you will alienate followers.

- *Research hashtags before creating/using them.* Some hashtags may seem straightforward and have a singular reference in your mind, but a quick search may turn up some surprising results. For instance, on Twitter, #myRA does indeed provide some posts on the US Treasury Roth program, but it also shows posts regarding people named Myra! Carefully consider all interpretations (with upper and lower cases, and a mix of both) to check for unintentional meanings or references.

- *Use unique-to-you hashtags wherever possible.* If you do create a tag that's unique to your organization, be consistent in its use to gain traction with all your followers and clients. Also, don't make it so unique or unusual that people cannot remember it.

- *Be judicious.* One or two tags per tweet or status update is sufficient. Tag keywords that people will actually search. Be strategic to yield the greatest impact. Don't use more than two hashtags in your tweets. Any more, and the tweets look like spam.

- *Tag complete ideas.* Separately hashtagging terms, such as #financial #solutions, won't categorize your content successfully. (Do you know how many "solution" bits of content exist on the Internet?) Don't use punctuation or spaces within your hashtag. Tagging #financialsolutions greatly increases the chance of reaching your tribe.

- *Placement.* A hashtag may be placed anywhere within a sentence. It can be a postscript (Great game! Another victory! #Dodgers), or it can incorporated within the text (Great game. Another #Dodgers victory!).

- *Use hashtags to create listening channels.* Consider a regular basis for terms such as #401k, #finances, #money, and so on. There are many words that individuals use when describing their financial life. Listening in on those conversations via Twitter may provide some ideas for your client outreach or content creation.

Hashtags allow you to sort through the Twitter noise. For instance, #retirement actually searches the whole Twittersphere and allows you to see just those tweets that have that #retirement in them. So it takes the billions of conversations going on in Twitter-world and helps you block out the noise and review what's happening right now. Imagine that you've tweeted the message, "Happy Birthday, Harold." Only your followers will see "Happy Birthday, Harold." However, if you tweet "#happy birthday Harold," people who have filters set up to follow #happy will see your tweet to Harold.

Twitter also lists trending hashtags. On some occasions, users will take a trending hashtag and try to figure out how to use it in their tweets in a purposeful or humorous way. Let's say the United States wins the gold medal in frisbee, and maybe you want to write a blog post about frisbee's similarity to investing. You could say, "#GoldMedal #Frisbee Ideas for Your Portfolio." That's taking the news and using trending hashtags in hopes of getting more views and more followers—in other words, "newsjacking."

A Cautionary Note

This actually extends beyond Twitter. Needless to say, be careful what you say via the social sphere. Take it from the ad exec who tweeted an insult about Memphis, the hometown of FedEx, on the same day he was meeting with the global delivery company on its turf. The flurry of weigh-ins and apologies that followed made international news and served as a reminder to "think before you share or tweet." (He also lost his job.)

Granted, you can delete your tweets (just as you can your posts on other social media), but as we all know, once something is said (or tweeted), it's out there. You can remove a tweet from your account (along with any subsequent retweets), but if other users comment on your tweet (they quote your tweet in their own tweet), that's not yours to delete.

Twitter also lists the individual accounts you follow on your homepage stream (as you follow them). Be careful who you follow. It will reflect on you and your business. I came across a financial advisor in the United Kingdom who was following a variety of Twitter accounts connected to particularly inappropriate content—scantily clad women. Wowza! What was he thinking?

While You're Out There . . .

As one of the fastest-moving social media platforms on the Internet, there are a few extra cautions to take when it comes to Twitter.

- *Dealing with trolls.* Make no mistake: Twitter has plenty of trolls, plenty of horrible, truly mean people tweeting. And many people are concerned about whether to respond to negative backlash. When considering a response, review the individual's account:

- How many people are following that person? Why bother messing with an account that has only fifty followers?

- What else does that person's feed discuss? Is that person regularly negative and snarky? If so, a response from you will only feed the fire.

- If that person commented on a service issue, consider making direct, personal contact rather than a full-blown public response.

- *Security settings.* As with any social platform, be diligent with regard to understanding the security settings for Twitter. My account is set up so that anytime someone sends a tweet including my handle, @missfitts, I get an email and a text message.

- *Notifications.* You can also set up your account so that you get notified when someone retweets one of your posts. (As a side note: this is where Twitter can go exponential. Let's say you have three hundred followers, and one of those folks decides to retweet one of your posts. That person may have fifty thousand followers, which means you've just gotten a tiny bit more traction. This may lead to a few more followers headed in your direction.)

Getting Familiar

There are some interesting ways you can become familiar with Twitter. As I coach for all social platforms, start by just listening. First, investigate other advisors, financial professionals, and firms. Pay attention to their activity. Also, take some time to see who they follow. In addition, check out their curated lists (lists of specific Twitter users in a particular category).

In fact, while building your Twitter account, you can create lists of your own—some private, some public. To start, create a private list of your current clients and centers of influence. Lists allow you to easily reduce the noise and simply focus on a particular group for a span of time. Or, for a public-list example, create a list of respected economists. Then, once a day, or maybe once a week, simply pay attention to their activity. This approach might allow you to easily "curate" content without having to sift through the other noise from the full Twitter-verse.

Ongoing Engagement

Twitter is a 24/7 news source. It constantly calls for your attention and participation. Various social media experts advocate for ongoing engagement. This approach is particularly challenging if you've got work and life commitments.

There are many brands and thought leaders who use Twitter as a one-way broadcast channel, not an interactive engagement channel. Obviously, there are arguments that could be made for either approach. One particularly savvy social guru suggests dividing Twitter activity into three buckets: one-third sharing original content, one-third sharing and retweeting others' content, and one-third interacting and having conversations. I split it up similarly with creating, curating, and connecting by sharing original content, sharing other interesting content, and interacting with others.

If you use it merely for broadcasts, there are tools that allow you to set a series of outbound, broadcast tweets so you don't have to maintain your Twitter stream on an hourly basis.

As an example, use Mondays as a planning day, and set up a possible set of ten tweets for the week. Since the life of a tweet is extremely short and people are dipping their toe into the platform throughout the day (and night), you may want to set up your broadcast to send out the same tweet a couple of days apart at different times.

There are oodles of platforms that can help you find out when your tribe is online and help you look at the success of your posts: Buffer, HootSuite, SocialSprout, and my current favorite, CoSchedule.

Twitter tip: Prescheduled social updates might make good business and time-management sense. Two critical points:

1. Limit your duplicate posts to different platforms. No one wants to see the same post across three platforms.

2. Even more importantly, monitor daily events in the world and adjust your outbound schedule accordingly. The last thing you want is to be sending a cheery Tweet or post out to your community while a terrorist event or horrible disaster is happening.

As a financial professional, you'll find Twitter useful for several purposes. Obviously, you'll want to follow clients and prospects to get a view into their daily business life. Also follow your centers of influence. You'll get a glimpse into their marketing and content-development efforts. This provides a view of their daily world and also a way to support them in the social sphere through retweets of information or news about them. For example, you could give a shout-out such as "Jim Smith CPA has just been named one of the top CPAs in the XYZ region."

CHAPTER EIGHT ACTION STEPS

- Visit deconstructingdigital.com and download my "Ultimate Digital Gear Guide."
- Follow me at @missfitts to discover more about the world of branding, marketing, social media, and my home town of Portlandia.

CHAPTER NINE

Make Facebook Your Friend

Y ou might think of Facebook as just a place to catch up on what your friends made for dinner, where they went on vacation, or what currently annoys them. But Facebook can be an important part of your social media strategy, depending on your tribe.

The basics of Facebook are similar to LinkedIn and Twitter: when you set up your Facebook profile, you have a masthead, or what Facebook calls "a timeline picture," and your individual picture that shows up every time you do an update.

In much the same way that you use the other two platforms, when you're interacting with people on Facebook, you can choose to respond to a post so it can be a "conversation." And you can also tag an individual with your update. For example, if I post something and I'm hanging out with my brother, I can list his name, and he would get a notice of that update.

As with LinkedIn, you can request to be connected with someone. The difference is that Facebook lets you connect with anyone—even a stranger—whereas LinkedIn asks how you know the person. When you have a friend request from Facebook, that person connects to you. You may also connect with companies and brands on Facebook by "liking" them or clicking the familiar thumbs-up icon.

Facebook allows you to create an individual personal page along with a business page, and the business options vary, based on your business type. For most local and regional firms, the "local business or place" or "company organization or institution" options make sense.

Some people have been on the Facebook bandwagon for a long time, and they really seem to rock it. They have a large community, and they understand the difference between sending an update from a business and doing a personal update.

One potential way to reach your tribe is to join groups of people with a mutual interest, such as those at a breakout session at a conference. Or you may have discussions with family or friends through groups—for example, "I went to visit mom and dad last night and here are my pictures." But you might also be part of a professional group, such as Investment Writers of the Northwest.

Groups can be public or private, the latter meaning that you have to ask for permission to join. It can actually be a viable teaching platform, if used very thoughtfully and not too formally. For example, if you want to have a financial-literacy group on Facebook, then your point would be to have people join that group so they can ask questions and find resources to help them navigate their financial lives. And as you can with your Twitter lists, you can divvy up your friends or contacts and choose to share updates with only specific subgroups of your community.

Rocking Facebook

One of the plusses of Facebook includes the ability to connect with clients on a personal level: you can see posts and pictures of them with their grandkids or maybe photos of them on vacation. But even though you're learning more intimate details about them, it's very difficult to use the information for business purposes. You can't really say, "By the way, I noticed that you have grandkids. Have you thought about a legacy-planning program?"

However, if you are "friends" with your clients on Facebook, it is very easy to take what you've learned online into the offline world. As an example, consider calling people for their birthday rather than simply posting a note on their page. Send a card of condolences rather than a sad face in the comment section.

Facebook content skews toward the more personal, more human interest. When I'm on Facebook, the last thing I want to read about is financial, insurance, or portfolio stuff. I can't imagine seeing that stuff pop up in my feed and thinking,

Oh, I've got to read that. So it's hard to think about making content in the financial services arena that would feel like human interest. However, something such as, "How much does the tooth fairy leave for a molar at your house?" might work. Facebook demands a different way of thinking, beyond stocks and bonds and taxes and estate planning. Facebook is human and interactive and fun. Rather than pushing your content or purposeful marketing, consider using Facebook as a connection tool.

I have a friend who is particularly fabulous at Facebook. He asks questions about simple things, "Pancakes or waffles?" The discussions that follow are sometimes funny and always interesting. He posts pictures of his travels or asks questions about trends that he is seeing.

A more viable way to appear on Facebook with your business may be to comment, for example, on a recent volunteer activity. For instance, if your staff and clients just partnered on a Habitat for Humanity build, you may want to take pictures and post them to Facebook. If you support the Humane Society, you may want to share images of dogs that need adoption. Or if you're repainting your office, it might be kind of fun to kind of talk about how people voted on what color they liked. Reveal a bit of what is behind the curtain. You are likely to form real connections with people if you provide glimpses of your own personality.

Take a peak at the robo-advisor financial brands on Facebook for a bit of inspiration—Betterment and LearnVest, for example. Brands such as these have obviously spent time and energy figuring out what might really resonate with their audiences. You might learn from them by liking their pages and cyberstalking them for a while to see the subjects and imageries of their posts—and the responses they receive from their audience.

Match the Media

Facebook is extraordinarily visual; photos are good fodder for the platform. And people tend to be on Facebook after work hours, so daily posting is a necessity. In fact, one of my connections has made a commitment for a year of kindness. She posts a daily random act of kindness to her page and includes a picture. (She gives away random awards to people: best smile of the day, best parking job ever, etc.) That's her shtick, and it works.

Don't have time for engagement like that? Think of it this way: Would you hang up the phone if your client was talking?

Since Facebook takes on a different tone from other social media sites and is more visual, you don't want to create content for Twitter and then try to use it on LinkedIn and Facebook. That's something to keep in mind when you schedule postings via technology such as HootSuite or Buffer; you'll be saying the same thing across different social platforms, and if your audience is connected to you on all those platforms, they'll see the same update over and over again. That's a recipe for being ignored.

One of the challenges of Facebook is the constantly tweaking algorithms. While you may intend that all of your "friends" see an update, they may not because an algorithm change disallowed them from seeing it, based on the last time they interacted with a post of yours. Facebook's algorithms make it very squirrely to use for business. For instance, Facebook made three algorithm updates in 2015 that may determine whether your content stays afloat:

- *Update #1:* If users who don't post a lot of content want to spend more time reading their news feed, more content will display, some of which may be duplicate posts from the same source.
- *Update #2:* Updates from close friends appear higher in the news feed.
- *Update #3:* Stories about friends "liking" or making comments to posts appear lower in the news feed, if they appear at all. [28]

If you opt for a business page, you may be even more challenged. In this particular case, you may opt to get in front of your tribe through Facebook's "boost a post" feature. This pay-for-exposure option ensures your post gets viewed by everyone who's liked your page. The cost depends on how many viewers you want to reach.

---

28 Lindsay Kolowich, "Facebook Updates News Feed Algorithm to Balance Content from Friends vs. Pages," HubSpot, April 21, 2015, accessed September 18, 2015, http://blog.hubspot.com/marketing/facebook-updates-news-feed-algorithm.

Combating these changes, according to HubSpot, means focusing on crafting better (instead of more) Facebook posts and beefing up your website content so that more people want to share your pieces on their personal Facebook pages instead of "getting on Facebook only by publishing on behalf of your brand."[29]

CHAPTER NINE ACTION STEPS

- Visit deconstructingdigital.com to download my "Ten Tips for Facebook and Your Business."

---

29 Ibid.

CHAPTER 10

The Dynamic World of YouTube

The social world is visual. Nowhere is that more evident than at another powerful platform: YouTube. The power of video was validated when Google bought YouTube in 2006. Today it's the second-largest search engine in the world and a valuable avenue to feed the Google beast.

YouTube is an ideal platform to create thought leadership and share your smarts, particularly if you're more comfortable talking than writing. What better way to validate your expertise than with a video of you speaking to a large digital audience?

An example of the impact of YouTube: I have a fairly limited YouTube presence right now with just a handful of videos (one of which is my dog getting whipped cream at Starbucks). Yet, through one of these videos, I was able to get a training project worth $40,000 from a very well-known mutual-fund organization. A man who ultimately became a client found my video through an online search. He watched all my videos, and then he contacted me because he found out that I specialize in the digital arena. He took my Social Selling Bootcamp and then secured me to do a social selling class, in person, for a team of thirty-four people. All of that came from one, eighteen-minute video.

YouTube Uses

What could you record and upload to video? Let's start by looking at this from the educational perspective. Just as with the other platforms we've discussed, think about what smarts you want to share with your tribe. What valuable, relevant content can you share? Maybe you want to create videos that simply define financial terms, or maybe you could answer frequently asked questions. How about explaining the benefits of a well-thought-out will or different kinds of trusts? Or you could, perhaps, create a ten-part presentation series on YouTube—for example, *What Every Baby Boomer Needs to Know about Social Security*. Creating content requires that you step away from what you know and step into the shoes of those who know nothing about the world of financial services. Take note of the terms that confuse them. Pull apart the complexity of our world into small, bite-sized ideas. Be a teacher rather than a salesperson.

The other day, I was on a plane with a woman. She was very clear about the fact that she now needs to take care of not only her finances but also her mother's finances. She had question after question about Social Security and about the donut hole in Medicare. What would happen from a tax perspective if her mom were to deed the property to her, and how would that impact her financial life? Having a video series for the tribe this woman belongs to would likely draw viewers.

How to YouTube

Even though I've done several videos now, I still don't feel comfortable doing them off the cuff. So I start by drafting a script, which helps me get around the "what-am-I-going-to-say?" issue. I try to make the script very conversational and ensure it's in my voice, and I practice the script by saying it out loud. (As a side note, you'll want to get your script approved by compliance before filming your video. That is likely to save time, money, and the sad state of refilming.) Once I'm ready to go, I work with a videographer who uses a teleprompter. That device lets me look straight at the camera, as if I'm talking to the audience, but allows me to read from the script. Using a teleprompter takes a little practice, but it is a magical tool.

You should be able to find a videographer in your area. Some studios are even set up for you to just show up, and everything is ready to go. There are also numerous, talented, young people able to edit your video for a fairly low cost. You may even want to check with your local college or university.

My videographer uses a "green screen." When you are filmed in front of a blank green screen, your image can be superimposed over any kind of background. It's what TV weathermen use. It's how they're able to continually change the background maps and graphics that they use to show the weather.

Using a green screen gives you a chance to really get creative. If you're talking to people about their retirement and financial security, you know they're dreaming of an awesome future, so maybe you could dress up in ski gear and have your video editors put a mountain behind you. Or you could be standing on a beach. Or you could be skydiving out of a plane. Think Hollywood. Think entertainment. There are so many possibilities.

If you prefer, you can just shoot videos directly from your laptop or your computer these days. This tends to produce more casual videos, and the results are just fine. (In fact, I'm investigating this approach as well. It's a much quicker means of production—and much less expensive.) Besides, even your computer monitor's video capability is ten times better than the video cameras we had a decade ago.

If you're doing a straightforward video, be sure to project what you want the world to see. If you wear Tommy Bahama shirts at all of your client meetings as a way to remind people of their retirement futures, then wear a Tommy Bahama shirt in your videos, not a suit and tie. It's just a matter of having a consistent personal brand. Again, your physical presence in the social space is just like your voice: it needs to be authentic.

When you upload your videos to YouTube, make sure you describe your video content and add in all those tasty keywords. Again, YouTube is the second-largest search engine in the world.

You can also take the content that you've created for YouTube and embed it on your website. Having video content on your site gives people another way to get to know you. The article "Marketers Have Lost Control of Insurance Buying Process" in the *Insurance Journal* talks about the world of online content development and how people look to validate their purchasing decisions before they even contact the seller. According to the article, "The typical consumer will visit, on average, ten places online before contacting an insurer or agency."[30] Think about how a YouTube video series could help you be more human, personal, and passionate for prospects who might be coming by your website while doing their research.[31]

Prior to uploading videos and embedding them on YouTube, you'll need to create a "channel." That is the singular location where you'll house all of your videos. It's fairly easy to set one up: You just open a YouTube account and customize the look of the channel by choosing a background, color scheme, and a few other aspects of it.

---

30 Andrew Simpson, "Marketers Have Lost Control of Insurance Buying Process," *Insurance Journal*, August 18, 2015, accessed September 19, 2015, http://www.insurancejournal.com/news/national/2015/08/18/378634.htm.
31 Ibid.

As with the other platforms, use your YouTube channel to drive people back to your website. You can turn suspects into prospects into opportunities into clients through the search function on YouTube. Each and every video you post via YouTube should have a call to action to point folks back to your website or a phone number to call.

Now, the cautionary piece of this puzzle is that when your YouTube video is done playing, viewers will be shown additional content, and you can't control what that content might be. If you've got a pretty prolific channel and people watch it regularly, over time they'll just be presented with only your videos. But it's possible that another video could pop up from a different financial professional. Unfortunately, some other video could show up that you wouldn't necessarily deem appropriate, and worse case, it could be somebody slamming financial services.

Beyond YouTube

You can use other hosting solutions that are not YouTube. For example, for some of our clients, we post videos on YouTube to drive and feed the Google beast. Then we upload those videos to a private video service, such as Vimeo or Wistia. We brand the videos, and then we use them on the clients' websites. In this way, we're getting our clients the YouTube bang for their buck, and we are also controlling the brand experience when visitors come through their websites. (Wistia and Vimeo have various subscription platforms.)

Videos, typically, link to players via video links on a landing page of your website. For example, if you head to www.shoefitts.com/speaking, you'll see videos that display on my website but that actually take you to YouTube.

You can easily create content from webinars you're conducting via Citrix GoToWebinar, WebX, Adobe Connect, or other webinar platforms. In addition to streaming your webinar live, you can record it and repurpose the content by uploading the recording to YouTube. Webinars are a great way to interact with people online. But remember, a one-hour webinar, max, should always suffice. We've all been on webinars where the speaker strays too much or drones on too long.

The world of online education is exploding, through portals such as UDME, Lynda.com, CreativeLive, Skillshare, and even Harvard University. Interestingly, in addition to building your digital brand, this option could be a revenue stream. Bottom line: Video is here to stay. What smarts do you have to share? Where could you go with video?

Don't Just Check the Box

Some advisors have heard they need video and they need a website. In an effort to check the box, they head to ready-made website creators that offer a low-priced website with a selection of videos. These are particularly generic in their approach. They are not targeted to your specific niche, they do not have your face or voice in the imagery, and they do nothing to feed the YouTube/Google beast. I'm not a fan. I'd rather see you sitting in front of your high-resolution computer camera and sharing a financial word of the week before spending time on a generic video (that I can watch on two thousand other websites).

Don't Be a Nag

I have a friend named Ernest, whom I deeply respect. He's an old-world kind of guy who has seen and done it all, but he isn't a know-it-all. He'll dispense advice but only when asked and only if he has a definite answer. Ernest has been happily married for forty-one years. I recently asked him, "What is it about your wife that makes you so happy?" He replied immediately, "She isn't a nag."

Ernest was joking—I know his lovely and fun wife—but his words actually contained sage advice that relates to how people are starting to feel about information and marketing.

We've been in the everything-digital landscape long enough that we're tired of being bombarded with information. We are done with the maelstrom of advertising, not only on every bus and bottle cap but online too. Everyone, everywhere, is nagging us. It's just too much.

So how do you get your message out to the right people without being a contributor to the information overload? Again, be very specific and intentional with your messaging and communications. Know what you want to say and whom you're saying it to.

And keep in mind that since 2014, video has grown by leaps and bounds. Blog posts with videos gain three times more inbound links than text-only posts. Clients and prospects want to see you in action. Being timely with your videos means not just making them apply to current articles and topics. It also means you must create them quickly, and most importantly, keep them the appropriate length. People may click out of a video if the counter reads longer than a couple of minutes.

It's not difficult for advisors to integrate this mind-set—less generic, more custom—into their social media strategy. Evaluate your current online approach and search out the opportunities to get specific using resources, tools, or simply a unique voice and targeted message. In the world of short- and long-form content, one platform isn't necessarily better than the other. It really depends on your audience—and what you're trying to say.

CHAPTER TEN ACTION STEPS

- Visit deconstructingdigital.com to download my "Video Best Practices Tip Sheet."

CHAPTER ELEVEN
Publishing and Podcasting

I f video is somewhat like creating your own TV channel, then some of the other ways to use the digital world are like creating your own newspaper or newspaper column or your own radio show.

It is mind numbing how many new platforms enter the market on a constant basis. I'm not going to go into them all at length because a fair number of them are challenging from a compliance perspective, most often dealing with content embedded in graphics. However, more and more archiving companies are creating ways to support the necessary compliance requirements.

The key with new platforms is to gauge—as best you can—their viability for the long term. For instance, people are still scratching their heads over Google+. Even as I write this book, the requirements with Google+ are changing. In short, right now, Google+ seems to be a stepchild of the social space, and by the time this book is published, it might be completely gone. Or it might be absolutely blowing the doors off. Until we know, I plan to keep tabs on Google+ simply because it feeds the Google beast.

Visual Platforms

A picture tells a thousand words. A picture can be memorable and very sharable. While Facebook, Twitter, and even LinkedIn are becoming more and more visual, there are two platforms that have visuals at their core: Instagram and Pinterest. These platforms might be difficult to translate into the world of financial services because their content is composed largely of pictures and videos, graphics and infographics. (Instagram is photos and videos only.) The Pinterest audience tends to be female. The audience for Instagram tends to be young, and those who can crack that tribe and get a visual strategy might be really successful. If I had a millennial tribe, I would be all over Instagram. Frankly, I should step up my Pinterest and Facebook game for my podcast *Women Rocking Wall Street*. Given the demographics and nature of these two platforms, it would be a very beneficial strategic play. Alas, there are only so many hours in a day. (Curiously, I already get 4 percent of my web traffic from Pinterest!)

Just as hashtags work on Facebook and Twitter, they also work on Instagram. Instagram is a mobile-only platform that allows you to upload a photo and place it on both Instagram and Facebook. It is tough to push traffic from Instagram to your site. Comparatively, Pinterest is a particularly fabulous avenue for "referral traffic" (traffic that is driven back to your site). And as you'll learn in the next chapter, creating an avenue to bring people to your website is a crucial component of the digital world.

Again, these platforms haven't necessarily been used very effectively by the financial services world, because they are wholly visual. Imagine the visuals you could create to teach people about the world of investing. For example, on Pinterest, you might create graphics that show how one small shift in expense control can effect a shift in savings. How might imagery make cash management fun? On Instagram, you might use a picture of a pile of pennies to demonstrate small changes. Or maybe you can create an infographic that explains international investing or socially responsible investing. Using visuals to explain dollar-cost averaging would be a lot easier than using the written word.

On second thought, don't! Who really wants to learn about dollar-cost averaging on a social platform?

In the financial services world, we say that compounding is the eighth wonder of the world. But a visual showing how compounding works for you or how it works against you as it pertains to debt and credit. People might get a better understanding of how it eats away at their income if you paint a vivid picture for them.

Even more fun? Use the Pinterest platform to work alongside your clients to create a vision board of their future. What might retirement really look like? What a lovely way to encourage them to dive deeper into their dreams. (Some would call this an intention board.)

Another visual platform, SlideShare, allows a way to upload multipage presentations such as photo slideshows or PowerPoint presentations. SlideShare is owned by LinkedIn, so once you've created a presentation via SlideShare, you can easily link it to your LinkedIn profile. Some experts continue to point to an opportunity with the SlideShare platform, specifically for referral traffic and thought leadership.

Audio Content

Another realm in the world of digital is podcasts. They can be video but are most commonly audio. Podcasts, which typically sound like talk radio, are gaining in popularity, particularly with *Serial* and *This American Life* and a couple of other multi-episode programs. For example, Dave Ramsey, known as Mr. Financial Peace, has a huge following of people. He started on the radio, but now he also distributes content via podcasting.

Podcasting is a fantastic way to get your content in the palm of your prospects and clients and get permission to be in their ear buds for thirty to forty-five minutes a week. If the average American commute is twenty-two minutes each way, imagine being the radio station commuters choose to listen to on a weekly basis.

Certainly, podcasting is challenging from the perspective of compliance because you likely need approval before you post, and it's usually considered to be static content. Having your prospects and clients voluntarily listen in each and every week may make the effort extremely worth while!

There are a number of platforms for podcasts. Listeners can subscribe directly from iTunes if they have an Apple phone, or if they're on an Android, they can listen in via Stitcher Radio or other apps. Apple has recently made the podcast app impossible to delete from the iPhone, a plus for podcasters. Your podcast can also be posted on your website and distributed through RSS feeds. A simple Google search will produce free classes and other resources to help you create your own podcast.

My podcast *Women Rocking Wall Street* has been going strong for more than a year now. My audience has grown slowly but surely, with nearly fifteen thousand downloads already! Given this success, I've launched a companion podcast to this book, *Deconstructing Digital*. This will allow me an audio platform to continue to help the financial services world embrace the digital sphere and prepare for the next-generation client.

Your Business as a Media Business

The digital world allows you to shift your thinking related to marketing. Rather than the static, one-way marketing, cold-calling world of the past, you might begin to consider marketing as media. You can be a publisher or a movie producer. You can have an education channel. You can publish e-books and put them on your website or on Kindle. And importantly, the same piece of content can be subtly modified to fit on each particular platform. A webinar I host and record can be posted to YouTube, translated into audio for a podcast, transcribed into a blog post, scrunched down into an infographic, and more. The digital world provides so many avenues for you to get the word out, and when done intentionally, it's amazing how that effort starts to multiply.

CHAPTER ELEVEN ACTION STEPS

- Visit deconstructingdigital.com for a copy of my "Five Easy Ways to Repurpose Your Content."
- Visit womenrockingwallstreet.com to listen in to my podcast.

CHAPTER TWELVE

Tying It All Together

In the previous chapter, I talked about the term *referral traffic*. This involves using the web to drive visitors to your website—again, your business's digital front door.

Actually, your website is beyond your front door. It is your digital office. It is the starting point for most of the content for your social media efforts. Content that serves the Google beast, content that solidifies your expertise, and content that, when shared in the social world, drives traffic and clicks back to your site.

At one time, many social media speakers cheered folks to jump in and join the conversation, to drive engagement. In fact, we compared social media to a cocktail party. The social world was, initially, considered a place where people didn't just show up and start selling; rather, they just checked in and shared a little of themselves.

But the social sphere is significantly more than just a cocktail party. It actually should drive particular activities that relate to business return on investment—website traffic, lead generation, and brand awareness. And sharing your smarts is how you drive those activities. If your only intention is to chit-chat, you likely won't drive traffic back to your website, thereby wasting your time and energy. Granted, that is a bit extreme, as there are ways to drive awareness and relationships without constantly forcing folks to your site. However, every once in a while, a link to your site is critical.

And listen up. You don't want to build your prospect base by social media alone. If you don't have a system set up to welcome visitors and add them to an ongoing nurture campaign, you're building your business on rented property. Social sites can (and will) change the rules, meaning that you have zero access to all of those fabulous people who like your Facebook page. Poof! All of your hard-earned connections erased.

Lead Magnets

Imagine a virtual magnet placed on your site, something that draws people in and helps them stick once they're there. That something is called a lead magnet. In addition to the already-valuable content on your website, a lead magnet is something of super, extra value such as an e-book, white paper, tip sheet, webinar invite, or a guide on year-end financial planning—

some kind of free nugget or *supercalifragelistic* information so irresistible that visitors think, *Oh yeah, I want that.*

But wait. Before you deliver that spectacular content, you request a bit of information, such as the visitors' names and email addresses. Once they click submit, an email is fired off with the valuable tidbit you promised. This functionality is called an autoresponder. Many email engines, such as Constant Contact or AWeber or MailChimp, have this basic capability available. Even better, once the automated system responds to your visitors' requests and delivers the lead magnet, it adds them to an assigned email list. You want them on your email list.

This simple little process can welcome visitors and, ultimately, nurture them from visitor to suspect to prospect to client . . . well, with a bit more work.

For instance, one of the lead magnets I use is *100 Tips for Social Media Success.* I advertise this e-book front and center on my home page. When people come to my site, they're free to grab a copy. But first, I request their names and email addresses. Once they do that, they're added to my email list. Then I regularly send them news and updates about social media, marketing, branding, and so on. This used to be called a drip-mail campaign, but I call it a nurture campaign because you're providing value over time by sharing your smarts and building your influence. (Besides, drip doesn't sound very comfortable.)

I know, I know. You may not still be not convinced about the email piece of what I'm saying because we're all on email overload. However, know this: email marketing is twice as effective as cold calling, networking, and trade shows and four times more effective than social media alone.

Think about this: today, the average sales process takes 22 percent longer than it did five years ago.[32] During this wait time, you can't just continue to knock on people's doors and say, "Buy from me." You'll just annoy them; they'll shut you down. But if you instead say, "Here's value," then you'll stay top-of-mind with them. Over time, they may actually give you a call when they have a financial trigger point and they need some help. In fact, depending on your email engine, you may be able to see who is opening those messages; you may even want to call on those who repeatedly open your emails, since they are obviously interested in what you have to say. The term many people use is top-of-mind awareness. Right? That is what you want.

This digital nurturing is also a perfect place to add people who've told you, "Not right now," or "I'm happy with my firm." Through an ongoing outbound process, you stay in touch. And someday, just maybe, they'll get fed up with their current firm and head out to look for a second opinion. (Remember most people decide to purchase after multiple touches. And many salespeople give up after the first one.)

---

32 Rob Peterson, "37 Facts on the Future of Social Selling vs. Cold Calling," biznology, December 22, 2014, http://www.biznology.com/2014/12/37-facts-future-social-selling-vs-cold-calling/.

Your nurture-campaign emails don't need to be superlong or complicated. You can provide a quick synopsis to content that exists on your website. That way, if folks like your content and they read it, they may stick around to learn even more.

Content: What to Say?

If at least 20 to 25 percent of the time that you're out there doing social media you bring people back to your website, you'd be doing pretty well. The content you create in the social space is yours alone and nobody else's. However, social media also allows you to share content from other platforms, which is known as "curating content."

I talked about this a little bit earlier, but let me expand on curating.

In my gentrifying neighborhood in Portland, Oregon, there are a few resale shops on the main drag. One shop is beautifully curated, meaning that all of the trinkets and treasures have a particular air about them. They seem to go together in style, esthetic, and even color. The store is filled with a particular freshness and vibe. In fact, it doesn't feel resale at all. It could easily be a straight-up, hip, retail shop. Three doors down is another resale shop. This one isn't as lovingly curated. Things seem haphazard in their selection, almost as if the buyers were simply tossing things together. And I'm simply not a fan. I have zero desire to step into the cacophony of that store.

And what does this have to do with content? Your social curating should be equally as focused and considered. Let's go back to the ideas we explored in chapter 4: once you know your tribe, have clarified its persona, and have identified your superpower, you'll have a starting place for sharing your smarts. What might you select from your interaction with the world that might help your tribe members navigate theirs?

In fact, in the social world, this idea of curating doesn't only help you stay ahead of the content-creation effort, but it also helps limit any tendencies to be overly promotional. If you're constantly promoting just your own content, people may see that as being selfish. I don't necessarily agree with this reason. Social media moves so fast, I'm not sure anyone notices these details. Nonetheless, curating content makes active participation in the social arena a little bit easier. And since the content doesn't reside on your website, and you've got your archiving systems in place, no compliance review is needed in advance—for most firms anyway.

Curating can help you become a thought leader. It demonstrates that you read, you're thoughtful, you're curious, and have opinions regarding various topics.

Until I launched ShoeFitts, I didn't have a website and couldn't have my own blog. This makes sense since I was working for another firm, another brand. As such, all I was able to share in the social world was *curated* content. Even so, I was able to build the thought leadership around the social arena because of how active I was and also because of the manner in which I shared content.

As an example, let's say you find an interesting article in *CEO* magazine. Maybe you found an article to be particularly inspiring, interesting, educational, even entertaining, or perhaps you find the content somewhat distressing. Either way, given your role, you're likely reading content across a variety of media that informs your worldview. A simple way to begin curating content is to share what you read and what sparked your interest or shifted some of your thinking. The key to curating is to include your own perspective on the article or content.

You likely have centers of influence that publish content as well. Read and share their content; promote their efforts in your social network. There's nothing better. Everyone likes the sound of their own name. (An added sales benefit? You're staying on top of important business relationships at the same time!)

The goal, as you're curating, is to develop a brand perception and to have your personal brand be perceived as you intend it to be perceived.

If you're very serious and professorial, the content that you opt to share might be very complex, with your translation included. Or maybe you really enjoy inspirational quotes. If so, why not create your own series of quotes around money and publish those?

Begin at the Beginning

When I am not traveling for work, mornings find me walking my dog, aBoo. We hike up to Mount Tabor Park in Portland, Oregon, an amazing urban landscape of huge trees and quiet trails. One morning, near one of the park entrances, I paused to watch as a rock wall was being installed. The landscape crew was about halfway through the project and was working to fit huge boulders into their proper places. As I observed their work that morning, I admired the ways these "stone quilters" created structures that were both functional and beautiful.

My admiration stemmed from an awe of their precision in placing those stones. They used guidelines and level lines to guide their efforts. But because nature is unpredictable, there was no exact plan guiding which rock to place first, second, third, and so on. In order to make their beautiful walls, they simply needed to lay the first rock, review the space, and then select the next one. They prepared as much as they could—piling similar-size boulders together, for example—and then they began. As they built, they tweaked, moved, and added smaller rocks to help create the wall they saw in their mind's eye. But such a wall could not exist until those first stones were laid.

For some advisors, social media is something like that stone wall. Social media seems complicated and overwhelming. But rather than beginning to lay a foundation on which to build, they opt to simply stand on the sidelines and watch others venture forth. Sadly, those advisors standing on the sidelines miss out on important conversations, critical connections, and an inexpensive way to build their brand, scale their marketing, and increase sales.

No more excuses! What's the first rock that you plan to lay to start your social media effort? How about something as simple as connecting with all of your clients and prospects on LinkedIn? Look for LinkedIn groups in your region or join your alma mater group. Make this week the week in which you set up a Twitter account or the week when you begin to integrate LinkedIn into your sales and marketing efforts. Whatever it is, begin by setting those first stones.

Set an intention to get involved, and dedicate time each day to integrate social media into your face-to-face networking and sales efforts. Here are a few ideas to help you get started:

- Look up each one of your clients on Facebook, LinkedIn, and Twitter. "Like" or follow their company pages.
- Do the same for your key partners or leaders in the financial services industry. You can learn quite a bit from their posts and discussions.
- Connect with other financial professionals outside your region. This increases your network and may provide a tipping point to your profile on LinkedIn.
- Before your next meeting, head to LinkedIn and review the profiles of the key decision makers.

- If you appreciate what someone posts in an update, comment on it. Or even better, share it with your network or retweet it on Twitter.
- If you watch CNN or listen to NPR regularly, add them to your Twitter feed or Facebook friends list.
- Finally, set a timer for fifteen minutes every day to explore social media. That way you won't worry about distractions, and you'll have a definitive deadline for your efforts.

Again, Consistency Is Key

As I mentioned earlier, it's important to be consistent with your message. Be sure to review the messages on your website, social media postings, newsletters, presentations, training materials, and so on. If you find inconsistencies, fix them. Then go through the same evaluation with each product or service you offer. Are you consistent with all the touch points of each? While you'll want to keep in mind your overall value statement, consider each element under that umbrella one at a time so you can stay focused.

Consistency in business not only helps your branding but can also help you be more productive. Author Robert Cialdini says our brains use consistency and commitment to establish regular cues and reactions to simplify our lives. So take that cognitive desire and apply it to your blogs and newsletters.

Think about what you can really produce, write down your plan (which our brains consider a commitment), and be consistent. Maybe you write one blog a month and send a newsletter every six weeks. Sure, you might prefer a blog a week and a newsletter every month, but if that's not realistic, stick with what you can do on a regular basis.

CHAPTER TWELVE ACTION STEPS

- Visit deconstructingdigital.com and watch my quick little video, "Understanding the Digital Ecosystem."

CHAPTER THIRTEEN

Let's Explore Together

S o now we've talked about what it means to have a digital presence. But just as nobody can be a jack-of-all-trades, you can't build a really solid presence on all the platforms by yourself. If you had a team, you could assign somebody to the various social platforms. But social media moves so fast that it is a challenge to be really effective on multiple platforms.

Instead, pick one place to be and get started. As a financial professional, I recommend starting with LinkedIn. If you're already there, be sure your profile is optimized. Or if you've already ruled out LinkedIn but haven't committed to another channel, start evaluating where else you should be. Remember that it's important to feel comfortable with one channel and see some successes before moving on to another channel. Here are a few takeaways that we've discussed:

- Financial advisors have a company and a personal brand.

- The website is home base and needs relevant content.
- You must continually drive people to your website.
- Don't discount email newsletters.
- Teach and share, and they will come.
- There's value in videos.
- LinkedIn, Twitter, Facebook: pick one.

On some level, I'm sure you already understand this idea of social capital because it's a little like money in the bank. Participating in the digital sphere will raise your social capital: if you give your smarts away, digital allows you to scale your message, to do not just one-to-one but rather one-to-many communication, thereby increasing your social reach and, quite possibly, your social capital.

Nobody Is an Expert

I'm not an expert. I'm an explorer.

Remember what I said earlier: nobody is an expert on everything social. It simply moves too rapidly and changes too often for anyone to immediately master every nuance of each platform.

When the digital world first started, we took our physical world of marketing and transferred it wholesale to the digital world. We just took our standard, printed newsletters and turned them into HTML. They had the same look, with pictures, mastheads, and articles. And we turned our paper brochures into our websites.

That approach is outdated. Unfortunately, some firms aren't able to break away from the physical world.

I was in sales before there were GPS systems. My Thomas Guide was a necessity to find my way around. Now I've got a Google Maps app that lays out directions to most everywhere I want to go. As an explorer, I can't wait to see what's going to happen when someone figures out how to make a Google Maps for my financial life. Everybody wants that these days. Tell me where to turn, or give me my options and let me decide. That's what people are craving.

Progressive organizations, digital-first organizations, are asking themselves, "What can we give people that will help them and that they can hold in the palm of their hand?"

People also crave purpose; something retirees and millennials have in common. The opportunity to create content and resources to answer that need is why I love digital technology. It offers the opportunity to reach so many people on scale. What if I were able to create some app to help a single mom navigate her financial life better? That would be spectacular!

And even though I do digital every day, I can feel overwhelmed. My emails act like rabbits and multiply every five minutes. Still, financial advisors, of all people, understand the power of compounding. So imagine shifting your use of the digital world by 1 percent a month.

If you're participating in the social realm with the wrong intent and the wrong attitude and the wrong tone, yes, you could stub your toe. But if you have good intentions now, in the offline office, why would you change that when you get online?

I invite you to follow me on Twitter, @missfitts, where you'll find some of my lists. Take a look and subscribe to a few. In particular, subscribe to my list of social advisors. This will allow you to see what other financial professionals are doing. Visit deconstructingdigital.com for more ways to navigate the vast digital realm, or visit my website, shoefitts.com, where you can subscribe to my mailing list and download other helpful information and tools.

Again, I'm not an expert. I'm an explorer. Let's keep exploring together.

ABOUT THE
AUTHOR

Financial industry influencer. Popular social media speaker. A creative force in financial- services marketing. And it all started when Sheri Fitts was five, selling her very own homemade rose-petal perfume in baby food jars, door-to-door.

Sheri Fitts is known as a "social media guru" and a "social-selling expert" and has been invited to speak about digital marketing and social media at countless financial-advisor and industry meetings. As a digital native, she's been quoted in numerous articles and is considered an industry trendsetter.

Today Sheri infuses ShoeFitts Marketing's educational programs, marketing packages, and speaking engagements with plenty of her early entrepreneurial flair. She debuted in the financial services industry as an award-winning graphic designer, progressed to participant-curriculum design, and advanced to sales and marketing before stepping out on her own as a consultant and speaker.

With twenty-five years of industry experience in her pocket, Sheri collaborates with retirement-plan advisors, third-party administrators, and financial services organizations to help them leverage marketing tools, social media strategy tactics, and meaningful connections. She has received awards and recognition from the Plan Sponsor Council of America, Pension and Investments; National Association of Government Defined Contribution Administrators; and the International Association of Business Communicators.

A natural-born communicator, Sheri also earned Toastmasters' adult-level Speechcraft certificate in the eighth grade. Now she's an award-winning speaker and has been named one of the one hundred top influencers in the retirement planning (DC) industry.

If all of that isn't enough to pique your interest, Sheri was also named Papergirl of the Year (1976). So you can be confident that when you work with Sheri Fitts, she delivers.

CPSIA information can be obtained
at www.ICGtesting.com
Printed in the USA
FSOW03n1633190416
19445FS